DATE			

WITHDRAWN

BAKER & TAYLOR

WILLIAM MARSHAL

MEDIEVAL ENGLAND'S GREATEST KNIGHT

WILLIAM MARSHAL
MEDIEVAL ENGLAND'S GREATEST KNIGHT

Myra Weatherly

MORGAN
REYNOLDS
Incorporated

620 South Elm Street Suite 384
Greensboro, North Carolina 27406
http://www.morganreynolds.com

WILLIAM MARSHAL: MEDIEVAL ENGLAND'S GREATEST KNIGHT

Copyright © 2001 by Myra Weatherly

Picture credits: The Library of Congress

Library of Congress Cataloging-in-Publication Division

Weatherly, Myra
    William Marshal, medieval England's greatest knight / Myra Weatherly.
        p.cm.
    Includes bibliographical references and index.
    ISBN 1-883846-48-X (lib. bdg. : alk. paper)
        1. Pembroke, William Marshal, Earl of, 1144?-1219--Juvenile literature. 2. Great
Britain--History--Angevin period, 1154-1216--Juvenile literature. 3. Knights and
knighthood--Great Britain--Biography--Juvenile literature. 4. Regents--Great
Britain--Biography--Juvenile literature. [1. Pembroke, William Marshal, Earl of,
1144?-1219. 2. Knights and knighthood. 3. Great Britain--History--Angevin period,
1154-1216.] 1. Title.

DA209.P4 W43 2001
942.03'4'092--dc21
[B]

00-048751

Printed in the United States of America
First Edition

For
Jonathan Carter

Contents

FRANCE AND ENGLAND
IN THE 12th CENTURY

SCOTLAND

NORTH SEA

IRELAND

ENGLAND

NORTH
WALES

♦ Nottingham
♦ Sherwood
Forest

SOUTH
WALES

London
♦

Canterbury ♦

ENGLISH CHANNEL

FLANDERS

NORMANDY

♦ Paris

CHAMPAGNE

BRITTANY

FRANCE

ANJOU

ATLANTIC OCEAN

BURGUNDY

POITOU

♦ Poitiers

AQUITAINE

TOULOUSE

GASCONY

MEDITERRANEAN
SEA

SPAIN

FOREWARD

HISTOIRE DE GUILLAUME LE MARESCHAL

Much of what is known about William Marshal comes to us from a long poem written after his death.

In 1219, William Marshal the younger commissioned a troubadour named John to write an account of his father's remarkable seventy-two-year life. The *Histoire de Guillaume le Mareschal* (*History of William the Marshal*) is a Middle French poem of 19,214 lines in rhyming couplets written on 127 parchment leaves. Discovered in the late nineteenth century, it is the earliest surviving biography of a layman in European history. Although the *Histoire* is unique in its content and aims, it falls in the tradition of French epics and romances dating back to the *Chanson de Roland* (*Song of Roland*).

The *Histoire* had no printed circulation during the Middle Ages. John created the epic poem to be sung for the Marshal's sons and daughters so that they would know "the great merits and the honor of their ancestor." During the Middle Ages, the troubadour's song was the main form of communicating news, history, and legend. They could be found everywhere, from the courts of kings, to the tournament grounds, to the hearths of peasants.

John had been acquainted with the Marshal when the great knight was in his prime, but the troubadour relied primarily on information provided to him by John of Earley to write the *Histoire*. The Marshal's dearest friend and squire related firsthand the experiences he recollected in the service of his master. He also shared the stories his master told him when he was alive. The troubadour spent seven years interviewing, researching, compiling the material, and editing the work. Apart from the *Histoire,* the Marshal's own charters—at least sixty-seven scattered in archives across Ireland, Britain, and northern France—shed light on his later career.

"The story of his life ought to encourage all good men who hear it," sung William Marshal's thirteenth-century biographer.

CHAPTER ONE

SENTENCED TO HANG

William Marshal was sentenced to death when he was five years old.

The year was 1152, and the death sentence imposed on young Marshal was only a minor incident in the long, bloody struggle between King Stephen and Empress Mathilda that ensued after the death of King Henry I of England. Henry's only son had drowned in 1120, and the dying king had left all his possessions to his daughter Mathilda. Earlier he had forced the powerful English barons to recognize Mathilda as the rightful heir to the throne and had then married his daughter to Geoffrey, the fifteen-year-old son of the Count of Anjou. The new husband was promised that the crown would pass to him through Mathilda. When Mathilda gave birth to a son, the future King Henry II of England, on June 3, 1134, it seemed that the old king's succession plans were definite. Henry I died believing that he had arranged for a transfer of power.

But when Henry I died in December 1135, many of the nobles had second thoughts about following the old king's instructions. Many of the nobles did not trust Geoffrey and Mathilda, who had rebelled against Henry I before his death because Henry had not signed over land and castles to them quickly enough. This breech between Henry I and his appointed heirs made the nobles nervous. How would the grasping couple rule when they had unlimited power?

During the impasse following the king's death, Mathilda's cousin, Stephen of Mortain and Boulogne, the greatest land-owner in England, took advantage of the nobles' hesitation and seized the throne. Stephen was crowned on December 22, 1135.

King Stephen enjoyed a short period of peace because Geoffrey and Mathilda were busy dealing with problems in Anjou and other parts of western France. But in 1138, several English nobles joined the couple and rose up in rebellion against Stephen. The long civil war had begun.

The war started off badly for King Stephen. He lost the Battle

of Lincoln and was taken captive. John the Marshal, William Marshal's father, was then a fearless warrior of King Stephen's court. His duties as marshal put him in charge of keeping order among the king's forces and making sure that the proper monies were dispersed to maintain the army. But, when Stephen was held cap-tive and his army struggled to survive while awaiting his release, John the Mar-

Henry I (above) intended for his son-in-law, Geoffrey of Anjou, to succeed him on the English throne.

shal decided to move over to Mathilda's forces.

John Marshal soon discovered that leaving King Stephen's army might not have been a wise move. West of London at the Battle of Newbury Castle, Mathilda's forces had little food or supplies and were barely able to withstand the initial attack. John knew they would not be able to hold out for long. He asked King Stephen, who had since been ransomed and had rejoined the fight, for a one-day truce to obtain permis-

King Stephen took young William Marshal hostage.

sion from Empress Mathilda to surrender the castle. King Stephen, who wisely did not trust John, demanded a guarantee that his former marshal would keep his word. Stephen demanded one of John Marshal's sons to hold as a hostage. His son would be executed if Marshal did not keep his word.

John Marshal chose William, his youngest son, to be the hostage and sent him over to Stephen's camp. But that night, instead of meeting with Mathilda and arranging for surrender as he promised, John reinforced his garrison with fresh troops and food. The next morning, he refused to surrender.

King Stephen was outraged. His advisers demanded that the traitor's son be put to death. Who would ever fear the king's word again if he did not follow through on his threat? But Stephen could not believe a father would be so cruel to his own son. He decided to give John another chance to surrender.

Again, John Marshal declined the offer. Stephen was familiar with the old man's determination. Earlier in the war, John had refused to abandon Wherwell Abbey even after King Stephen's men set fire to the church. Flames licked the top of the building and molten lead splashed down from the roof onto his face, destroying one of his eyes. Now the defiant warrior's battle-scarred face showed no emotion when the king's messenger reminded him that his son would be sacrificed. John replied: "I possess the anvil and hammer with which to produce many more sons." King Stephen was left with no choice but to order the hanging.

King Stephen ordered the gallows built in full view of Newbury Castle. The next morning at sunrise, the procession marched to the execution site with King Stephen leading the way. Little William Marshal, who did not realize that he was walking to his death, playfully asked to swing in the load basket of a large catapult that had the power to hurl a huge boulder 200 yards. Some of Stephen's knights suggested killing the boy by hurling him over the castle walls from the catapult.

As Stephen watched the cheerful little boy skip along the path to his death, he was filled with remorse. Swooping him into his arms, King Stephen vowed, "William, you will never be harmed by me."

Maybe John Marshal knew that his former master would never execute an innocent child. Or maybe he truly did not care if his son died. The king withdrew his forces from Newbury Castle, but he continued to hold William prisoner for his father's treachery. John Marshal continued in the service of Mathilda and Geoffrey.

Back in camp, King Stephen kept the little prisoner in his tent, not so much for the child's safety as for his entertaining prattle. Young William played around the royal encampment, running in and out of the woods at the edge of the dense forest. Hounds yapped at his heels.

One day, William wandered the encampment picking *plantain*, a weed with spiky leaves. He returned to the king's tent with big bunches of the weed in each hand and asked Stephen to play "knights" with him. The boy and the king each took a plantain and began to mock battle. The player whose "knight" struck off the head of his opponent won. In the first round, to William's delight, he delivered a blow that whacked off the topmost clump of leaves from King Stephen's plantain.

As they sat on the floor enjoying the mock tournament, William glimpsed someone peering through the folds of the king's tent. His mother had sent a young servant from the Marshal's household at Marlborough to see how her son fared. William shouted with joy at seeing the familiar face: "How is my lady mother? How are my sisters and brothers?" Terrified by the boy's unexpected outburst, the servant fled and narrowly escaped capture.

William stayed with King Stephen until Empress Mathilda gave up the fight and returned to Normandy in 1148. Before she left, Mathilda arranged for her son, the future Henry II, to be left in England under Stephen's care. King Stephen, who did not have a son, also promised that Henry Plantagenet would be the heir to the throne. At the end of the conflict, King Stephen returned young William to his family at Marlborough.

No one knows how William Marshal felt about his father's willingness to see him hanged. There did not seem to be any ill feelings between father and son. In the Middle Ages, only firstborn sons received the family inheritance. As the fourth-born son to his father's second wife, William probably expected to have to fend for himself. Maybe being a hostage to King Stephen served the boy as a lesson for how he would have to live his life—by the use of his wit, intelligence, charm, and fighting skills.

CHAPTER TWO

KNIGHT WILLIAM

William Marshal was born eighty years after William II, the Duke of Normandy, invaded the island-nation of England and defeated the English Saxon King Harold at the Battle of Hastings in 1066. William the Conquerer was then crowned King William I of England. The Normans were the most feared fighters in all of Christendom, and soon after conquering England, they dispersed throughout Europe selling their well-honed killing skills to the highest bidders.

When William was twelve years old, his father arranged for him to go to Normandy to receive training as a knight. The training he would receive would provide him with valuable skills he could sell to the king or other barons. It was one of the few choices of professions available to a young man who did not have land or money to inherit. The young boy stuffed a woolen sack with his belongings and said good-bye to his weeping mother and sisters. Accompanied by two servants, he rode away from Marlborough and its gray hills cropped bare by thousands of sheep.

The England William left behind as he crossed the English Channel to Normandy had gone through great changes since he was held as a hostage by King Stephen. The kindly king had died in 1154 and as promised, Henry II, the son of Mathilda and Geoffrey of Anjou, was crowned king. At the time of his coronation, Henry II was only twenty-one years old. The ceremony had been a bedraggled affair. Westminster Abbey, the church where all English monarchs were traditionally crowned, had become dilapidated during Stephen's turbulent reign. In fact, all of England had suffered greatly during the civil war, and the people had grown weary. Henry II had ruled for five years when William Marshal left for Normandy.

Fortunately, Henry II's youth and vitality brought new hope to the people of England. His subjects came to love him for the energy he brought to the throne. They did not mind that the barrel-chested, freckle-faced redhead looked more like a countryman than a king. Despite his lack of a regal appearance, Henry was a scholar and was fluent in many languages. He loved debating as much as he did the hunt. He also had a fiery temper that soon became notorious. Once, Henry flew into such a tirade over a courtier's remark that he tore the covers from his bed and began to gnaw the straw mattress.

In his early years as king, Henry spent most of his energy reversing the ill effects of the past nineteen years. By the time of William's departure for Normandy, the phrase "merrie England" depicted the general mood of the country.

One person who was merrier than most was John Marshal. His valiant support of Henry's mother, Mathilda, had not been forgotten, and he had earned favor with the new king. He was rewarded with castles and land.

William the Conquerer defeated King Harold at the Battle of Hastings in 1066.

Henry II understood the limitations of a king's power in this feudal society. He realized that his power was not absolute. The king was more like the first among equals than the all powerful ruler that we think of today. Henry realized that to maintain power he had to control the other barons. He did this primarily by making them gifts of land and castles. The nobles returned the favor by supplying the king with soldiers and support when he needed to go to war. In a society grounded on the principles of war, fighting men were the most valued property in the realm.

In Normandy, William received the best possible military training. The Lord of Tancarville, his father's cousin, was known as the father of knights. For eight years, William worked as a squire, serving a retinue of ninety-four knights. Lord Tancarville supervised not only the training of his young relative but several other young boys as well. William was soon one of Lord Tancarville's favorites. The boy loved this world of cavalcades, armories, stables, and hunt.

Inevitably, some of the other squires became jealous of William. They complained to the sire that at dinner he received the finest pieces that left the pot, even before they got to the lord's plate. They gave him the nickname "scoff-food." Lord Tancarville ignored the gibes of William's detractors, and William endured the backbiting in silence.

William showed a natural flair for fighting. With the other squires of the castle, he practiced wielding weapons—the lance, the sword, and the shield. The lance was a long, pointed shaft of a tough, but lightweight, wood fitted with a metal tip. A knight secured the lance with one arm and held his shield in the other. He could then charge an enemy, knocking him from his horse with the long weapon.

FEUDALISM AND MEDIEVAL LIFE

Feudalism was the way political, social, and military relationships were organized during the Middle Ages in western Europe. Feudalism was built upon a relationship of obligation and mutual service between vassals and lords. A vassal held his land, or fief, as a grant from a lord. When a vassal died, his heir was required to publicly renew his oath of faithfulness to his lord. This public oath was called *homage*.

Feudalism in practice often meant that the country was not governed by the king but by individual lords, or barons, who administered their own estates, dispensed their own justice, minted their own money, levied their own taxes and tolls, and demanded military service from vassals who were trained as knights. Sometimes, such as during the revolt against King John in 1214, the lords could field greater armies than could the king.

The vassal was required to attend the lord at his court, help administer justice, and contribute money if needed. He must answer a summons to battle, bringing an agreed upon number of fighting men. As well, he must feed and house the lord and his company when they traveled across his land.

Medieval society was structured around a lord's manor where peasants farmed, artisans created handicrafts, and knights protected the lord's holdings.

The lord was obliged to protect the vassal, give him military aid, and guard his children. If a vassal's daughter inherited a fief, the lord arranged her marriage. If there were no heirs, the lord disposed of the fief as he chose.

Although the king was sometimes less powerful than the barons, in England it was assumed that all of the land belonged to the sovereign prince. The prince would grant fiefs to his barons, who made their oaths of homage to him and were required to give him political and military service according to the terms of the grant. The barons, in turn, might grant portions of their fiefs to knights who swore homage to the baron. A king might grant a baron twelve fiefs, for example, and then expect the use of ten knights to be provided by the baron. A baron could then give one fief to each knight in return for service. Or, the baron might seek to keep all his fiefs to himself and pay for the upkeep of his knights out of his own funds.

Medieval life was structured around the manor. A manor consisted of the manor house and one or more villages surrounded by thousands of acres of land. Some of the land was divided into strips. The goods produced on each strip were assigned to either the lord of the manor, the church, or to the peasants who worked the land. Time was also spent maintaining the common areas of the manor, such as roads and bridges, as well as cutting firewood, clearing land, and other chores.

The peasants who worked the land lived in rough huts that lacked chimneys, windows, and floor boards. One part of the hut might house valuable livestock, such as cows, goats, or oxen. Beds were softened with straw or dried leaves, and the furniture was usually limited to a few stools and tables. A peasant's diet consisted of porridge, cheese, bread, and vegetables such as turnips, onions, and peas.

William and the other squires practiced this technique, called *tilting*, with a target called a *quintain*. A quintain was a post with two arms that swung on a pivot. The target was affixed to one of the arms. A heavy sandbag hung from the other arm. The sandbag gave the target arm a weight similar to a human body. But it also added another dimension to the practice: After a squire hit the target with his lance, he had to continue riding at a full gallop to avoid being knocked off his horse by the sandbag that spun dangerously at his back. If a *flail*, or studded metal ball, were attached to the spinning arm, the squire's injury could be even more devastating.

The strenuous training hardened William's body. Although the chain-mail armor of the twelfth century was much lighter than the plate armor that was used in the late Middle Ages, it was not self-supporting. Instead, it hung awkwardly and heavily on the body. A squire required tremendous physical strength to maintain his seat astride a horse. Every squire had to learn how to leap fully armed into the saddle without touching the stirrups. Dressed in full armor, William built up his strength by running races, jumping ditches, and climbing walls.

These squires aid the knight with his horse and armor as he prepares for battle.

William and the other squires cleaned, polished, and tested their master's arms and armor. They also cleaned out stables and curried the horses. Learning to take care of his horse was an essential skill for the aspiring knight. His life would depend on his horse as much as his prowess.

Being a squire involved more than training for battle. At elaborate feasts, musicians entertained as servants carried platters loaded with food. William served his master as table squire—carving meat, cutting bread, and pouring wine. Because no one used forks, he carried a napkin over one arm so that the diners could wipe their hands between courses.

William also hunted in the forests surrounding Tancarville. He learned how to use a boar spear, how to track game, and how to recognize the signals blown on the hunting horn. He also mastered the art of falconry. Although these were considered the sports of kings and nobles, once his training days ended, William showed little interest in hunting or hawking.

As the years passed, William excelled in the more courtly graces. At Tancarville, he learned the rules of courtesy, the latest dances, and the popular games such as chess, backgammon, and bowling. From the troubadours, he learned to sing. Like most people in the Middle Ages, however, he never learned to read or write. In later life, he would employ clerks to keep his accounts.

At age twenty, William knew how to conduct himself among the court. He had mastered the fundamentals of his profession and had imbued the rigid code of honor and duty known as chivalry. He felt he was ready to test his skills on the battlefield.

His chance came in 1167. After eight years of peace, war flared again between King Henry II of England and King Louis

VII of France. The reason for the conflict and animosity was simple. Henry had inherited vast areas of France—including the provinces of Normandy and Anjou—from his father and mother, who had spent most of their lives in France. Louis wanted Henry's lands.

Although he was technically the vassal of the French king, his French holdings in addition to the crown of England made Henry II a powerful rival of Louis. This tension between the English ruler and French king, that sometimes resulted in conflict, would continue for centuries.

At the beginning of this conflict in 1167, King Henry II summoned Lord Tancarville to help defend the Norman camp at Drincourt. Tancarville gathered a small force of his squires and knights, including William Marshal, and set out to join forces with other English knights.

It was at this time, on the eve of his first battle, that twenty-year-old William was knighted. Lord Tancarville presented him with a new cloak and strapped a sword to his side. He bestowed upon William the *colée*, the ritual blow to the shoulder, and intoned: "In remembrance of Him who ordained you and dubbed you knight." There was no time to perform the full knighting ritual—a vigil, bath, mass, and feast.

The following day, William demonstrated the skill and tenaciousness that was to mark his career. The Normans met the Flemish and French forces at full gallop with thunderous clashing. Eager to prove his valor, William darted to the front rank. Tancarville cried out for William to get back and let the more experienced knights get through. William pulled on the reins. His stallion, hooves churning, skidded to a halt to let his elders pass. Then, despite the rebuke from his master, he spurred his horse on until he was in the front ranks again.

William fought with such savagery that his lance shattered under the force of his blows. He drew his sword and fought on in the narrow streets. From their windows, the Norman townspeople cheered him.

In the heat of the fight, William swung back from a charge to find himself facing thirteen French soldiers. He was trapped. A soldier snared his shoulder with a four-clawed iron hook that was used during peacetime to pull burning thatch from houses. As the soldier dragged William from his horse, thirteen iron links of his chain-mail shirt gave way. William struggled to his feet and removed the hook, but his wounded horse died on the spot.

The townspeople hurried from their windows and armed themselves to aid the Norman knights. After the citizens of Drincourt joined the melee in the streets, the French withdrew.

Later that evening, the Norman knights celebrated their victory. As the wine flowed and the revelers discussed the battle, the Earl of Essex asked Marshal for a gift. "Give me a crupper or least an old collar," the Earl teased.

This request for pieces of horse tackle puzzled the new knight because, as he explained, he had never owned such things in his life.

"Oh, but Marshal, what are you saying? You had forty or sixty of them—yet you refuse me so small a thing?" the Earl responded. Boisterous laughter erupted in the hall. Embarrassed, William admitted that he had unhorsed many knights in his efforts to save the town but had failed to seize their steeds or to hold them for ransom. The Earl's joke taught William the important lesson that war was fought as much for gain as for honor. It was a lesson he would never forget.

Soon after the battle, Henry and Louis signed a truce that

ended the war for the present. The chamberlain and his knights headed for home. William sold the rich *mantle*, or cloak, presented to him at his dubbing for just enough to buy a baggage horse. He returned to Tancarville with only his sword, his torn shirt of chain-mail, his cloak, and his nag. He had not gained much booty in his first conflict.

A few days after William's return, news reached Tancarville of an upcoming tournament at Le Mans. The mid-twelfth century tournament was much different from the kind popularized in today's movies and books where armored knights fight individual jousts. The individual joust became the centerpiece of the tournament more than a century later, resulting from the efforts of religious and political leaders to make the events less dangerous.

The typical twelfth century tournament was usually a small affair. Two informal teams, made up of a score or two of professional knights, competed. Although the knights fought with the same ruthless skill in the tournaments as they did on the battlefield, they did not try to kill one another. The tournament offered an arena to practice for war without the threat of death. A knight was worth more alive than dead. Still, because of the inherent danger, knights did die during the competitions. Sometimes there were prizes offered to the winning knight, other times the victors were allowed to keep any captured spoils, such as horses, weapons, and armor. Defeated knights could also be held for ransom.

At the beginning of the melee, two groups of mounted knights attacked one another across fields or along village lanes. In larger tournaments, the melee spread over several villages or filled miles of countryside with the clang of swords, the grunts of knights, and the snorting of winded horses. The battles could last for days.

At his first tournament, Marshal longed to capture some of the necessities of knighthood that he had failed to get at Drincourt. But his only horse was the baggage drey he brought back from battle. He could not enter the competition without a worthy mount.

As the Lord of Tancarville and his court prepared for the tournament by polishing arms and adjusting saddles, bridles, stirrups, and shield-straps, William agonized. Eventually, the chamberlain took pity on his young kinsman and provided him with a mount—one that no one else wanted. The horse looked splendid, but other knights had found him too wild to train. William leaped into the saddle and the horse shot off like an arrow trying to buck his rider. William quickly gained control of the steed and with a little work soon had the horse obeying his commands.

At his first tournament, William proved his prowess in combat, restored his finances, and began his journey into legend. He quickly captured three knights, including Philip de Valoigne, who was the most elegantly armed knight on the field. He was then attacked by five knights who struck him with the flat of their swords. One

The helmet that William Marshal pried from his head at his first tournament probably resembled this one.

blow caught his helmet and twisted it back to front on his head. Near suffocation, William retired to the sidelines with his winded horse. In the process of breaking the thongs and removing the helmet, he severely cut his hands. His companions pleaded with him not to reenter the fray, but Marshal ignored them. He donned a fresh helmet and dashed back into the melee. He was the most gallant knight of the tournament, and at the end of the day, he received a prize: a magnificent war horse from Lombardy, a district in what is today northern Italy.

Now that he had tasted the glories of battle at Drincourt and won a tournament, William wanted to see his family. He decided to return to England. On the eve of his departure, Lord Tancarville warned William that primitive, backward England was no place for a knight seeking advancement on the tournament circuit. Normandy and Brittany, on the west shore of France, were the best places to be a tournament knight. But Marshal longed to return to the land of his birth, and he boarded a ship for England.

CHAPTER THREE
SERVICE IN A ROYAL HOUSEHOLD

William returned to England in 1167 a handsome young warrior. His athletic figure was so well formed that it might have been "fashioned by a sculptor. His face even more than his body resembled that of a man of high enough rank to be the emperor of Rome."

John Marshal had died in 1165, and his remains lay in a tomb at Brandenstoke priory. Although William had not seen his father since he was twelve years old, he always remembered his bravery. William's brother John had inherited the now substantial estate and the position of marshal. William had to fend for himself.

He called on his mother's brother, the wealthy Earl Patrick of Salisbury, asking for a position in the nobleman's *meinie* (military household). In mid-twelfth century England, kings and great barons employed hundreds of knights to protect their land and interests. These knights often came from mixed backgrounds and shared a fondness for war.

Because word of William's battlefield skill had already reached England, Patrick welcomed him. He was preparing a campaign to the French province of Poitou, where Henry II's subjects were rebelling and destroying the king's properties. William joined his ranks, and the young knight was soon again bidding farewell to his mother. He then set sail across the English Channel for the province of Poitou.

Henry had acquired Poitou through his marriage to one of the most beautiful and brilliant women of the Middle Ages. Tall and slim, Eleanor of Aquitaine had married King Louis VII of France in 1137. Louis was a serious and pious man; Eleanor was younger, lively, and more intelligent. Although Louis adored his young wife, problems developed in the marriage. These tensions were aggravated when the couple failed to produce a male heir.

In 1146, Louis decided to go on a Crusade to the Holy Land as part of his Christian duty. Eleanor also "took the cross" and accompanied her husband. On the trip, she was accused of flirting with a variety of men and of having an affair with one of them in the city of Antioch.

After returning to France in 1152, the marriage of Louis and Eleanor was dissolved, conveniently, on the grounds that they were distant cousins. Eleanor was fortunate that her husband was a compassionate man. He could have accused her of adultery, had her executed, and confiscated her lands. Instead, Eleanor returned to Poitou a wealthy woman.

To keep control of her lands, Eleanor needed to find another husband. Although he was eleven years younger than she, young Henry Plantagenet, as he was called for wearing a sprig of broom or, *planta genista*, in his cap, seemed to be just the man. Henry was also the heir to the English throne as well as to the provinces of Normandy, Anjou, and Maine. Eleanor had met Henry when he had accompanied his father to France to offer homage to

COURTLY LOVE

Courtly love was the ideal code of behavior for aristocratic lovers that developed at the Poitiers court of Queen Eleanor. The conventions of courtly love, which were influenced by chivalric ideals and feudalism, were passed along in the songs of the troubadours.

Most of the ideas of courtly love stemmed originally from the *Ars Amatoria* (*The Art of Loving*) by the Roman poet Ovid. According to these conventions, a nobleman, usually a knight, in love with a married woman of equally high birth or higher, had to prove his devotion by heroic deeds and by amorous writings presented anonymously to his beloved. Once the lovers had pledged themselves to each other and consummated their passion, complete secrecy had to be maintained.

Because most noble marriages were arranged by parents as business or strategic contracts, the type of true love valued in the songs of the troubadours was said to exist only outside of marriage. Eleanor herself said that although true love in marriage would be admirable, it was not probable.

Eleanor returned to her court at Poitiers in the south of France after she departed from Henry and reunited with her oldest daughter, Marie of Troyes, who had been born during her marriage to Louis. The court at Poitiers was soon dominated by Eleanor, Marie, and their ladies. The woman-dominated court reveled in the games of the courtly love tradition. They organized mock trials, where the judges sat on a raised dais and listened to the love songs of the troubadours before passing judgements on the love struck pleas of the finely dressed young courtiers.

Queen Eleanor became the model for the renewed interest in the Arthurian legends, particularly the sad story of Queen Guinevere's love for Lancelot. Marie requested that a new version of the romance be written and performed at Poitiers, where it was very popular. Marie also requested that a friend, Andrea Capellanus, write a treatise called *The Art of Courtly Love* to explain the rules. Among the conventions is the idea that courtly affairs involve a love that must be kept secret and chaste because the beloved is usually a married woman of higher social status; there should be extravagant praise of the lady; all that is good about the lover comes from his desire to be worthy of her; love always catches the lover unaware (sometimes with only a glance at his beloved); the lovers regularly stare into each other's eyes and faint, sigh, and burst into tears; lovers lose their appetites and grow pale and wan; and lovers discuss the nature of love endlessly.

The cult of courtly love flourished during a time when women, even of the aristocratic class, were considered to be little more than property. Eleanor and her daughter were attempting to raise the status of women by educating men in the nature of love. It was an effort to apply the code of chivalry, which governed how men behaved on the field of battle, to romance. While Eleanor may not have managed to alter the relationship between the sexes of her day, today the romantic notions of chivalric love have outlasted the more military aspects of the code. Although women remained second-rate citizens in medieval society, for a short time at the castle of beautiful Eleanor of Aquitaine, women were teachers to men. The notion that women could command over men was so subversive that it attained cult status.

But the idea did not last long. When Henry seized Eleanor and returned her to England as punishment for supporting his son's revolt, he disbanded the court at Poitiers. Henry was so angered by the idea of the court of love that the frightened Andrea Capellanus later denied writing *The Art of Courtly Love* and attacked Eleanor and Marie for their heretical ideas. But an ideal of true love that, at least in fantasy, freed aristocratic women from the position of mere property had been born, and it would take more than the rage of a frustrated monarch to kill it.

Louis. She never forgot her first glimpse of the young prince, pounding across a field on a foaming stallion with a falcon perched on his wrist. On May 18, 1152, eighteen-year-old Henry and twenty-nine year-old Eleanor were married in a cathedral in Poitiers, the capital of Poitou. In the summer of 1153, Eleanor gave birth to her first son, whom they named Henry. Two years later, Henry Plantagenet was crowned King Henry II of England, and Eleanor was again a queen.

Just as she had gone earlier with Louis on the Crusade, Eleanor joined Henry II on the mission to Poitou. King Henry assigned Patrick and his knights the task of escorting his wife to a safe castle. Patrick did not expect an attack and so took only a few lightly armed men, including William Marshal, with him.

The unsuspecting group was attacked by a brigand of disloyal subjects. Patrick managed to get the queen to safety, but before they could mount an attack, he was driven through by an enemy sword from behind. Earl Patrick died before his nephew's eyes. Enraged, William jumped on his horse and charged the enemy— forgetting to put on his helmet. He struck right and left with his sword, hacking at his uncle's murderers with ferocious strength until the assassins knocked him from his horse.

With his back against a hedge, William continued to fight "like a wild boar amongst the dogs." He stood the Poitevans off until one of them sneaked behind him and drove his sword through the foliage, slashing William's thigh. William did his best to bind the wound with the straps of his leggings and to continue fighting. But his garments were soon soaked through with blood, and he collapsed.

His captors tied William to a mare and hurried him off to be held for ransom. They bundled the disabled knight from hiding place to hiding place, waiting for the ransom money to be paid and disregarding the wound in his leg.

Nights later, while the rebel band rested at a friend's castle, a lady noticed the prisoner's wound. After being told of the youth's courageous acts to avenge his murdered uncle, she hollowed out a loaf of bread and filled the hole with shredded linen. Then she sent the loaf to William who proceeded to dress his wound. The lady's kindness probably saved his life.

One evening, as he had just begun to heal, William agreed to a stone-throwing contest with one of his captors. William beat his opponent by a foot and a half, but he reopened his wound in the process. Despite a few bright spots, William suffered during his capture more than any other time in his life. He was shuttled from hiding place to hiding place in excruciating pain because he had no horse to ride. He had to settle for any donkey or mule that could be found.

William resisted despairing that no one would ransom him. Finally, Queen Eleanor heard of William's plight. He had risked his life to protect her, and his beloved uncle was dead in her service. She bought his freedom and his loyalty. Queen Eleanor, the richest heiress of Europe, was the ideal patroness for a young knight, and soon William was her favorite. At age twenty-one, William had joined the Plantagenet household. Only one year after being knighted, he had achieved every young knight's dream—service in a royal meinie.

For the next fifteen years, William served the Queen. She showered him with presents: horses, arms, money, fine clothes, and all the equipment a knight needed. In turn, William was generous with his wealth. He freely dispensed money to his friends and followers. He had learned the value of having the support of his comrades was more important than riches.

King Henry II remembered well the difficult years that preceded his ascension to the English throne. The bloody civil war between his mother and King Stephen had barely secured his birthright, a right Mathilda never acquired for herself. Henry wanted his son to be anointed as the king as well as heir to his domains while he was still alive. This way there would be no question of who should succeed him. But, as the king would soon discover, this plan also led to destruction and grief. The coronation of the oldest Plantagenet son, Henry, was held in 1170. From this time on, the son of Henry II was called the Young King.

King Henry II of England ruled from 1154 until his death in 1189.

After the ceremony, King Henry selected William Marshal to be the Young King's military tutor. This was a high honor for the landless fourth son of a minor baron. Marshal had become the most respected military figure of his age. He was as well known for his honesty and integrity as for his skill as a knight. Now he was responsible for the training of a king.

When Marshal entered Henry's meinie, the Young King was fifteen years old, tall, fair-haired, charming, irresponsible, and extravagant. One day, on a whim, Young Henry ousted everyone who was not named William from a crowded banquet. Because William was the most common Norman name at the time, this left numerous guests at the table, including William Marshal.

Young Henry's household numbered as many as 200 people.

As chief in the meinie, William dealt with dukes, counts, and even kings. He was a constant presence around Young Henry's castle. He usually dressed in robes of yellow, green, and red silk, sometimes topped off with flashing jewels.

Royal courts were often filled with deceit and treachery, and the Plantagenet court was no exception. The older king had filled the positions at his son's court with honest men, such as Marshal. But the young, headstrong king surrounded himself with hangers-on with weaker morals. Many of them were crooks; others were intent on creating discord.

After three years of instruction from William, the Young King excelled in physical prowess and knightly manners. Financially, however, the spendthrift son continued to live off his father. He was a constant drain on the king's resources. Finally, Henry stopped granting his son's requests for money.

Young Henry's irritation with his father's financial restraints increased as his ne'er-do-well courtiers egged him on. To complicate the problem, his mother, Eleanor, was now estranged from Henry II. She spent her time at court in Aquitaine and often sent back messages encouraging the Young King's resentment.

Unfortunately for Henry II, his son had a powerful ally who stood to benefit from domestic troubles among the Plantagenets. When the Young King was only five years old, he had been married to three-year-old Princess Marguerite, the daughter of King Louis VII and his second wife. (In effect, the Young King was married to the daughter of his mother's first husband.) Henry II had intended for the marriage to help secure the Plantagenet's hold on their lands in France. Now, however, his plan was used against him. Eleanor joined her eldest son at the French court as the Young King asked his father-in-law, Louis VII, for support against Henry II. The French king was more than happy to create havoc in the household of his arch-rival.

Henry II was not without blame. While he had earned the love of his people, he could also be a dominating ruler and an infuriating father. He gave his sons, Henry, Richard, and Geoffrey, legal title to their own provinces and castles but refused to allow them any real power. After the Young King formed an alliance with the king of France, his brothers joined him in the rebellion.

This chasm between father and sons placed William Marshal on dangerous footing. He may have sympathized with Henry II, but the ties of feudal loyalty bound him to the Young King. He had been assigned to his meinie, and the rules of feudalism were clear. He should fight with his master.

The rebellion broke out in the summer of 1173. But the Young King had an embarrassing problem: He had not yet been dubbed a knight. Henry II had hoped to see his son knighted by his father-in-law, King Louis VII. Before the battle with his father began, Henry turned to his faithful mentor to perform the ceremony. William Marshal—a knight who did not own "an acre of land, or anything else save his chivalry"—girded Young Henry with the sword. Then he kissed the new royal knight in the presence of Young Henry's retinue.

The political goal of the royal brothers was to set the Young King on the throne of England. They had some support—there were always barons and other royalty who seized any opportunity to create trouble for a king, especially one as strong and domineering as Henry II. The conflict spread rapidly. King Henry II soon found himself so outnumbered that he had to resort to hiring mercenaries (knights who fought for money) in order to put an army in the field.

When the Young King and Louis first attacked Henry in Normandy, they seemed to have momentum on their side. But after two months of fighting and maneuvering, they were forced to retreat.

The conflict dragged on with little results. After a year and a half of strife, peace returned in 1174. The aging Henry II signed treaties with his sons and King Louis. He pardoned his sons and held no grudges against William. While the sons escaped punishment, Queen Eleanor was confined to a castle in Winchester. For fifteen years, Queen Eleanor was under house arrest. She saw her family only at Christmas-time.

At the end of the war, William accompanied the Young King to England. For a time, Young Henry enjoyed the peace, spending his time hunting and fishing. Still, he longed for the action of battle.

CHAPTER FOUR
Tournament Hero

William accompanied the bored Young King back to Normandy, the playground for knights, where infatuation with tournaments was at its height. They found a sponsor, the Young King's cousin Count Philip of Flanders, and plunged into the chivalric life of northern France. However, success on the tournament field was slow in coming to Henry's meinie.

After losing the first few tournaments, William advised his master to try a new tactic in the next game. He had the Young King pretend that he would take no part in the contest. Then at an opportune moment, William would lead the royal knights to attack their exhausted opponents and win. The plan worked.

Dating back to the eleventh century, various popes had condemned tournaments, but they flourished nevertheless. Participants and spectators came from France, England, and Scotland to Normandy. Passionate organizers (dukes, counts, and earls) spent lavishly to put on a great show. They fed their guests and offered prizes to the champions. The sponsors acted as a club. In some instances, the barons equipped whole companies of knights as Count Philip did when William and Young Henry's meinie turned up in 1176 lacking arms and war horses.

In one such tournament at Anet, William and his master had become separated from their men when 300 foot soldiers commanded by French baron, Simon de Neauphle, confronted them. Undaunted, William, backed by Henry, charged straight into their ranks and the soldiers gave way. William seized the baron's horse by the reins (his favorite way of capturing knights). They rode on through the town towing Simon behind. Deprived of his reins, the helpless Simon could only flail his arms until a low-hanging gutter knocked him to the ground.

When they reached camp, William, still leading the riderless horse, ordered his squire to take charge of the prisoner. When he turned, he saw to his amazement the empty saddle and the Young King bent over with laughter. William joined in the merriment made at his expense.

Large tournaments occurred less frequently. These elaborate festivals lasted for days. They took place across miles of open countryside that served as the knights' playing field. Rivers, woods, farmlands, vineyards, and farm buildings provided shelter and hiding places from which to launch an ambush. The winning team succeeded in either chasing the other team from the field or gathering the greater number of captives at the end of the day.

Few formal rules governed the tournaments. Knights relied on chivalric honor to assure rewards. Located throughout the countryside were refuges: roped-off areas set aside for resting and rearming. Breaking into these neutral regions resulted in heavy penalties. It was also bad form to slip away from a captor. But perhaps the most regulated part of tournaments concerned the taking of ransoms. The rules allowed for a group of pursuers to attack a lone knight or to take a wounded man prisoner. Once a prisoner paid his ransom, he was free to rejoin the field—if he were physically able.

The countryside between the towns of Anet and Sorel was the site of a tournament attended by Henry's meinie. They arrived late to find the knights of the Angevin lands—those controlled by the Plantagenets—facing defeat. Soon after the arrival of the Young King and William Marshal, however, the superior English troops were able to send their opponents scattering across the countryside.

Some of the fleeing knights scrambled to the top of an earth mound surrounded by a moat. Many of the fugitives left their horses tethered outside the palisade fence built on top of the mound. Sighting the horses, William dismounted, waded the moat, and scaled the mound. He grabbed the reins of two of the finest horses and headed back down the mound. As he was climbing up the bank of the moat, two French knights appeared, seized the horses from him, and galloped off. The French knights had broken one of the rules of the tournament: It was very bad form to steal horses taken fairly by another man.

Remounting his charger, William continued on his way. Soon he arrived on the scene of fifteen French soldiers holed up in a farm building besieged by a group of Angevin knights. The defenders (two were French knights of rank) offered to surrender themselves and their possessions to William. "You are more worthy of them than those who are bent on capturing us." Ignoring the objections of his own party, William let them go and refused all offers of ransom.

Following the tournament, William wasted little time finding the uncle of one of the men who took his captured horses.

CHIVALRY

The code of knightly behavior called *chivalry* came to prominence in the eleventh and twelfth centuries, flourished in the thirteenth, and gradually lost its hold as the medieval era gave way to the Renaissance, and chivalry was subsumed by an enthusiasm for gentlemanly behavior. During the Middle Ages, the knight was considered the champion of Goodness against Injustice and Evil.

Raymond Lully's *Book of the Order of Chivalry*, written in the thirteenth century, formalized much of the chivalric code. Among the basic tenets of this code for a knight were: 1) devotion to the Church and its teachings, 2) defense of the weak, 3) fearlessness in the face of an enemy and mercilessness toward the Infidel, 4) truthfulness and generosity, and 5) loyalty and chastity. Although a knight first owed his loyalty to God, he also devoted himself to his temporal master, or lord, and to his sworn love. In the chivalrous sense, love was largely platonic, and as a rule, only a virgin or a married woman could be the chosen object of a knight's love.

Medieval knights followed the code of chivalry in battle and at court.

Shocked at his nephew's misconduct, the Frenchman ordered the horse returned. Someone suggested that William give the young man half of the horse and then throw dice with him to see who should have the whole animal. William agreed and won the horse.

The second young knight who stole the horses was a member of the meinie of a French baron. Hearing William's story, the baron ordered his vassal to return the horse. Some thought the youth had a certain claim to the twice-captured horse, so William asked the young man to estimate its value. The youth, thinking that William would ask him to pay half of his estimate to keep the horse, priced the mount low at fourteen pounds. To his surprise, William threw seven pounds on the table and rode off with a horse worth a great deal more.

In one tournament, William successfully defended a prisoner against five other knights. He won a fine war horse for his efforts. At dinner following another tournament, William glimpsed an opponent lying down in the street with a broken leg. William "rushed outside, ran to the groaning knight, took him in his arms, armor and all, and carried him into the inn." He placed the injured knight in the middle of the table and said to his dinner companions, "Here, take him to pay your debts."

In 1177, word reached Young Henry's court of a forthcoming tournament at Pleurs. Because it was too long a journey for his entire entourage, the Young King sent William and a companion. They arrived to find the valley swarming with high-ranking officials. Mounted on their chargers, knights from as far afield as Spain and Sicily hoped to gain honor and profit. William distinguished himself once again on the tournament field. After his exploits at Pleurs, William Marshal became known as a sort of tournament superstar, much like a sports hero of today.

After the Pleurs tournament, the nobles gathered to discuss the events of the day. The lady of the castle presented a fine pike as a trophy to the Duke of Burgundy. He declined in favor of someone else. The fish passed from one count to the other— round and round the table. Then, the Count of Flanders suggested sending this strange prize to the hero of the day: William Marshal.

Two knights preceded by a squire holding the pike aloft set out to award the trophy to William. They found him at the blacksmith's shop, kneeling with his head on the anvil while the smithy pried off his iron helmet. William accepted the prize with becoming modesty. The envoys returned and told the story of finding him with his head on the anvil. The barons' admiration for William increased even more when they realized that William had continued to fight even though his helmet was smashed down on his neck.

Though an enthusiastic patron of chivalry, Young Henry could not attend enough tournaments to satisfy William. So in the spring of 1177, William teamed with another knight on a tour of all the tournaments. Life on the tournament circuit enhanced William's reputation and purse. During one ten-month period, William captured 103 knights.

One day at Joigni, before a tournament began, William sang as the knights and ladies danced. When he had finished, a minstrel sang a new tune with the refrain, "Marshal, give me a good horse."

William saw an opportunity he could not resist. As the first opponent cantered onto the field, he slipped away from the dancing throng. He mounted his charger, unhorsed the knight, and presented the captured steed to the minstrel. This impulsive act fueled his reputation for generosity.

After two years of traveling from tournament to tournament, William returned to Young Henry's household. No longer on his own, he resumed command of his master's meinie. Now in his thirties, William remained unmarried and landless.

CHAPTER FIVE

A FIGURE OF CHIVALRY

The largest and most extravagant tournament of William Marshal's lifetime took place in 1180 near Lagni, a city famous for its fairs. Three thousand knights swarmed the area, including companies of highly skilled mercenaries of low birth. The mob was swelled by a throng of followers: horse dealers, merchants, moneychangers, and courtesans. Estimates of the size of the crowd ranged as high as 10,000 people.

Because most people did not read or write, heralds traveled far and wide to the courts of patrons, towns, and villages announcing the upcoming tournaments. These professional informers perfected a system that enabled them to rapidly spread the news over vast regions.

People came from all over to watch the spectacles. The Duke of Burgundy and nineteen counts attended the Lagni event. Teams, grouped by nations and dressed in corresponding colors, their banners waving in the breeze, added to the pageantry.

Young Henry amassed a large multinational formation. Eighty knights from France, Flanders, and Champagne brought his total forces to more than 200 men. William was not part of Henry's team. At Lagni, William Marshal participated for the first time as a *banneret*, or the leader of a company of knights under his own colors. He adopted a banner that was half-green and half-yellow and featured a raging red lion in the tradition of the English kings.

Preceding the charge of the teams, youthful knights entertained the crowds by parading and jousting. Wearing ornate armor made specifically for the event, they galloped across the field toward each other with their lances poised.

The tournament at Lagni opened with the announcement of the names of the participants by the heralds. The heralds' job was to identify helmeted faces on the field by the heraldic signs on their shields. William had his own press agent, Henry Norreis. At the opening of every tournament Norreis cried out: "*Dieu aide au Marchal*!" (God Help the Marshal!)

Amidst the fanfare of trumpets, the armor-clad knights made their grand entrance astride their horses displaying rich trappings and harnesses. The sun glinted off their lances. Their banners fluttered in the breeze. Louder than the peal of thunder, the roar of war cries signaled the charge. Dust swirled as the onrushing teams pounded across the field, causing the earth to tremble. The splintering lances, cracking shields, splitting helmets, tearing asunder of hauberks, and tumbling horsemen added to the cacophony.

The troubadour named John, writing in the thirteenth century about William Marshal, described the tournament at Lagni beginning with the hubbub:

> Grand clamor and great noise
> All were eager to strike home.
> Here could you hear the clash

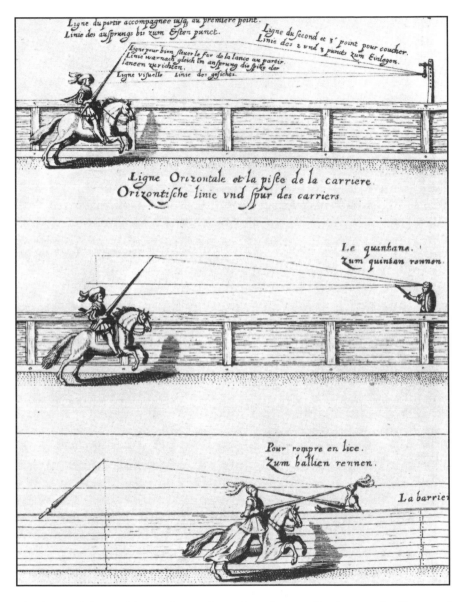

Ligne du partir accompagnee iuſq; au premiere point.
Linie des auſprungs bis zum Erſten punct.

Ligne du ſecond et 3.ᵉ point pour coucher.
Linie des 2 vnd 3 puncts zum Einlegen.

Ligne pour bien ſteuer le far de la lance au partir.
Linie warnach gleich im anſprung die ſpitz der lancen zurichten.

Ligne viſuelle.   Linie des geſichts.

Ligne Orizontale et la piſte de la carriere.
Orizontiſche linie vnd ſpur des carriers.

Le quintans.
Zum quintan rennen.

Pour rompre en lice.
Zum ballien rennen.

La barrie

This diagram, "The Art of the Joust," comes from a sixteenth-century French manuscript. The top and middle frames show the knight practicing with a quintain, and the bottom frame shows an actual joust.

of lance against lance, the pieces
falling so thick upon the ground
the horses could not charge.
Great was the press on the plain.
Each troop shouts its war cry

. . . .

Here one might see knights taken
and others coming to their rescue.
On all sides were horses to be seen
running and sweating with dread.
Each man eager to do all he could
to win, for in such enterprise
prowess is quickly seen and shown

. . . .

So mightily did William Marshal fight
that none of those who were there
knew what had become of the king.
Later on, the king was to say,
and all those who had seen him,
and those who heard speak of him,
that never was such a feat seen
or heard of from a single knight,
finer than the Marshal's on that day.
The best men praised him mightily.

The hordes of fighting men remained after the competition
ended, and the field took on the atmosphere of a fair. Merchants
converged to sell their wares. Colorful tents dotted the playing
field. The clink of money being counted replaced the clang of
arms.

William distinguished himself at Lagni by giving away his
winnings, but not before taking a squire named Eustace. He had

come a long way since being a childhood prisoner of King Stephen. Now a famous knight, William Marshal was on equal footing with counts and barons.

All did not go smoothly for William, however. Back in the Young King's court, his success and celebrity aroused the envy of five members of the meinie. The jealous courtiers concocted a plot to destroy their comrade by spreading a rumor that William had slept with Young Henry's wife, Marguerite. When word of the rumor reached him, William responded in the only way a chivalric knight could: He maintained a stoic silence, neither denying nor acknowledging the charge.

The titillating rumor ran rampant throughout the king's household. Then, as now, people had a taste for salacious gossip. The conspirators babbled to the Young King that they were informed of the rumor's truthfulness by both hearing and by sight. At first, the king refused to believe them. Then, he became so hostile that he no longer spoke to William. A few months later, Henry sent Marguerite to live with her brother, King Philip II of France, who was crowned after the death of his father, King Louis VII, in 1180.

William decided to leave the court. Soon afterwards, the Young King summoned William to attend the last tournament of the season in the autumn of 1182. William turned up fully armed. The desire to win overcame his shame and resentment. William surpassed everyone and twice rescued the Young King from being captured. Then King Henry and William went their separate ways.

Soon, William decided to publicly declare and fight for his innocence. He hastened to attend the king's Christmas court at Caen. When the king rejected his offer to fight three of his accusers, William proposed that a finger should be cut off his right hand and then he would fight the strongest of his enemies. If he failed in combat, the suspicious Young King could put him to death by hanging.

After his challenges were brushed aside, William felt he had but one choice: He must leave the Plantagenet lands. He feared that this was the end of his distinguished connection with the English royal house. It had been a valuable, if painful, lesson about how unstable success at a royal court could be.

Thirty-five-years old and still in his prime, William planned to turn to the tournament field and take the many lucrative offers that came his way. But first, in early 1183, William set out on a pilgrimage to Cologne in Germany. His goal was to visit what were supposed to be the relics of the Three Wise Men. He spread the word that by this holy journey he hoped to be cleansed of the suspicion of adultery.

Meanwhile, Henry and his brother Geoffrey launched another rebellion against King Henry II. This time, brother Richard supported their father. Young Henry, in need of funds as always, found himself up against a large army. Besieged in the castle of Limoges, Young Henry and his counselors decided that they needed the wisdom and valor of William Marshal on their side. The Young King sent for William to resume his position as commander of his troops. His men scoured the countryside until they found William returning from Cologne.

Before rejoining Henry's meinie, Marshal obtained, with the aid of letters from the French court, permission from Henry II to return to his son's rebel camp with the assurance that the charge of adultery would never be mentioned again.

On the way to join his former master, William arranged to

rendezvous with two knightly companions who were also returning to Young Henry's camp. Before reaching the meeting place, drowsiness overcame William. He stretched out in a sheltered spot by the roadside and dozed off. Meanwhile Eustace, his squire, put the horses out to graze and kept watch.

The sleeping knight awoke to sounds of horses and the murmuring of a woman saying, "God, how tired I am." William caught a glimpse of a couple riding by on two fat palfreys loaded with bulging saddlebags.

"Bridle my horse," he ordered his squire. "I must find out who they are." In his haste, William forgot his sword.

Catching up with the pair, William grabbed the man by the sleeve of his fine cloak and asked who he was.

"I am a man."

"I can see that you are not an animal."

Shaking off William's grip, the stranger put his hand to his sword.

William shouted to his squire to bring his sword. Quickly, the man covered his sword with his cape. Then William snatched off his hood and discovered that the stranger was a handsome, young monk.

The couple confessed that they had eloped. The girl revealed that she was Flemish and had no intention of returning to her country. Concerned, William asked how they were going to live. The monk boasted that he had at least forty-eight pounds in his money belt. He planned to lend the money and live on the interest. This idea shocked William more than their elopement. The Pope had condemned *usury*, the lending of money at interest, as a mortal sin. He ordered his squire to seize the money and then left the penniless couple behind as he hurried to join his waiting friends. When he met his two companions, William tossed the money belt on the table and divided the windfall. After feasting and hearing of William's adventure, the three knights set off on the long journey to Poitou.

By the time William reached his young master, the campaign was in serious trouble. Money had become short. Desperate for means to pay his mercenaries, the Young King had resorted to seizing treasures from monasteries. While on a pillaging expedition to a shrine near Martel, Young Henry fell seriously ill from an attack of dysentery. It was soon clear that he was dying.

Informed of his son's impending death, Henry II sent him a ring from his finger as a token of forgiveness. On his death bed, the Young King—crowned but never a ruler—made a public confession renouncing his recent acts against his father. Before receiving the last rite, he gave his cloak with the Crusader's cross to William Marshal, instructing him to carry it to Jerusalem. He requested that he be buried at the cathedral at Rouen. Clasping his father's ring, he lapsed into unconsciousness and died a short time later. William directed the preparation of the corpse for the long trip to Rouen. The embalmers removed the bowels, brains, and eyes. Then they packed the body with salt and stitched it into a bull's hide.

On the way to Rouen, a party of Spaniards blocked the procession of the cortège and seized William, demanding that he pay his master's debts. After much haggling, they agreed to release him for a ransom of 100 marks. Unable to pay such a large sum, William promised to surrender himself after he had escorted the body to Rouen. Hearing of the episode, King Henry II paid the 100 marks, commenting, "My son has cost me more than that in the past and I would that he were still an expense to me."

On July 22, 1183, the Young King was buried. His contemporaries mourned and wondered what they would do without their generous patron to furnish them with arms, steeds, and money. Without a benefactor, they now had to look elsewhere for a livelihood.

Setting aside his career, William prepared to keep his deathbed promise to Young Henry and take the cloak marked with the crusader's cross to Jerusalem to pay his master's debt to God.

These pilgrimages—or Crusades—were a series of holy wars fought by European Christians between the eleventh and fourteen centuries to recover the Holy Land from the Muslims. The religious zeal of the times and the lure of travel and adventure attracted every social class in western Europe. Kings and commoners, bishops and barons, and knights and knaves participated in the expeditions to the shores of the Mediterranean.

Nine major Crusades developed during this centuries-long movement. In addition, there were the ill-fated Children's Crusade and countless smaller, regional ones. The Second, Third, Fourth, and Fifth Crusades, as well as the Children's Crusade, occurred during William's lifetime.

Carrying a cross to the Holy Land was, for many, the ultimate service of a knight. William Marshal had shown his devotion to the crusades by contributing generously to the Knights Templar in his days of prosperity.

Custom dictated that a crusader say farewell to his friends and family. William made a brief trip to England to see his brothers and sisters. Many years had passed since he last saw them. He bequeathed to them his belongings as if he were preparing for his own death.

Before leaving England, William visited Henry II. The aging

king urged him to come back soon. He gave the crusader traveling money of 100 pounds. He also took two of William's horses as a guarantee of his speedy return to the royal court. The horses that the king kept were worth 200 pounds.

Then William Marshal took the cross on the road to the East, fulfilling his duty to Young Henry and to God. He would spend two years in the Holy Land before returning again to England.

Forming to battle for Christianity and recover the Holy City of Jerusalem in the East, the Knights Templar became a powerful organization that eventually challenged the authority of the western European kings.

THE KNIGHTS TEMPLAR

The Knights of the Temple Soloman, or the Knights Templar, was formed in Jerusalem during the Crusades when a small band of nine knights led by Hugh de Payens joined together to protect pilgrims to the Holy Land. Approximately ten years later, the Knights Templar was officially recognized at the Papal Council of Troyes in 1128. The Templars grew wealthy and powerful as they received gifts of estates and money from wealthy nobles, and the organization soon became one of the most powerful in Europe. Because of their role in the Crusades, the Templars were responsible only to the pope and thus reigned free from secular control.

Known as great warriors, the Templars could be spotted in battle by the red cross they wore on the breasts of their white tunics. In the later Crusades, tension between the Templars and other knight orders erupted in a deadly rivalry. This rivalry weakened the strength of all the crusaders.

By the end of the thirteenth century, the Templars had ceased to be primarily a fighting organization and had become the leading money handlers of Europe. As their banking role increased they served such kings as Henry IV of England and Louis IX of France—and as their landholdings grew, they aroused the hostility, fear, and jealousy of secular rulers and of the clergy as well. By 1308, the Templars were actively being persecuted. Members were tortured and forced to confess to various sacrilegious practices. The Papal Council of Vienne dissolved the order in 1312, and the Templars were completely destroyed by 1314.

CHAPTER SIX
LANDED BARON

On his return from the Holy Land in 1186, William Marshal met King Henry at his hunting lodge in Normandy. As a welcome to the now legendary knight, King Henry granted the Marshal a small fief and entrusted to his care the heiress Heloise of Kendal. Should he choose to marry Heloise, he would take permanent possession of her lands. William also received another ward: fifteen-year-old John of Earley. John served William as squire and knight, remaining his faithful servant for the rest of William's life.

William spent the next few years engaged in active military service. His time as a tournament knight was behind him. From this time on, he fought only in the service of his king.

These years were a bewildering maze of raids, sieges, battles, skirmishes, conferences, and truces between King Philip II of France and King Henry II of England. William confronted the French in battle time and time again. Most of these wars were fought as ravaging and quick attacks on strong-points. Extended, pitched battles were avoided. The intention was not to destroy the opponent's army but to surprise the enemy and destroy economic resources by pillaging and burning fields and destroying flocks.

At war, William Marshal was an "impressive military peacock" in his robe of yellow, green, and red silk. Under the flowing surcoat, he wore a fine-meshed mail hauberk and leggings. Beneath that, a padded under-robe lessened the shock of blows to his body. His steel helmet, gilded clasps, and jewels flashed in the sunlight.

Most of the fighting took place on the French side of the channel. In the spring of 1186, English forces occupied the town of Gisors. The French, including armed citizens, marched on the town. After much confusion and useless waste of life, someone suggested to King Henry that four knights from each side should fight it out, leaving the fate of the town to the outcome.

Messengers brought the plan to the French king, who agreed. King Philip chose four champion knights from his own army, and then, in jest, he chose four of Henry's weakest men, who were unfit due to age or infirmity, to fight for the English. Seething with anger at being ridiculed by Philip, King Henry exclaimed: "My lords, of what use are you? You are my counselors and you give me no advice."

William advised Henry to set the battle in a neutral court. He then suggested four worthy English contestants, including himself. At first, Henry's fiery son Richard protested at being omitted from the list. Thinking quickly, William responded that it would be unwise to risk the life of the heir to the throne in such an affray. In the end, however, both sides abandoned the idea, and the French continued to attack Gisors as unsuccessfully as they had before.

According to a popular story at the time, there was a beautiful elm tree, round and flourishing, just outside the town. It angered the Frenchmen to see Henry's troops resting in the shade of the elm, and they threatened to cut it down. Hoping to protect the tree, the English encased the trunk in bands of metal, but this did not stop the disgruntled French. One day, finding the tree undefended, the Frenchmen chopped the famous elm of Gisors into pieces.

Furious that his army had achieved nothing more by its attack on Gisors than the cutting down of a tree, King Philip asked, "Are we an army of woodcutters?" Disgusted, he disbanded his men.

The Marshal advised Henry to appear to do the same but issue secret orders to reassemble in a few days. "By God's eyes," said the king, "Marshal, you are most courteous and have given me good advice. I shall do exactly as you suggest."

William's plan worked. The English swept over the border, burning fifteen villages and amassing a large amount of booty. When Richard praised his father, Henry noted, "We have well avenged our elm tree and this is due to the good and loyal advice of the Marshal."

Henry ordered William to continue the devastation of the enemy's land. In the skirmish to capture Montmirail, William was on the outskirts of the town while the struggle went on inside. Informed that the army needed his help, he shouted to his squire, "Bring my shield!"

By the time William reached the town, the enemy had retreated to the castle, leaving ten armed soldiers, one mounted, on the crest of the narrow bridge that spanned the moat. William flicked his reins and spurred his charger on until he came face to face with the defenders of the bridge. The French turned their spears on William's horse and badly wounded him. The horse turned around and fled with William still on his back. Both the horse and William arrived safely at the bottom of the steep slope.

Had he fallen from his horse into the deep moat, nothing could have saved him. His comrades criticized his rash actions. He admitted that seeing the one knight on horseback made him long to seize the bridle and take him prisoner as if they were on the tournament field.

By the spring of 1189, all attempts for a lasting peace had failed. The king's relations with Richard, his heir, were no more

This thirteenth-century picture shows William Marshal unhorsing a foe.

satisfactory than they had been with Young Henry. Old King Henry II had more problems. His son Richard believed the rumors he had heard that his younger brother John was Henry's choice for heir. Angrily, Richard left the English camp and joined the French. King Philip II had won Richard over to his side the same way that Louis VII had influenced Young Henry against his father.

When William informed the old king of his son's treachery, he said: "I knew only too well that my children were destined to destroy both themselves and me. They have caused me nothing but grief and shame." Once Henry II had described his

HENRY II AND THOMAS BECKET

The tragic conflict between Henry II and Thomas Becket forms the basis for one of the most famous stories in western history. Their great friendship was torn apart by political conflict, the root of which was the tension between church and state. This tension is still a hot topic in the world of today, and this story of an English king and an archbishop has since become the subject of plays, novels, and movies.

Thomas Becket, born the son of a London merchant, began his career as a deacon for the archbishop of Canterbury. The archbishop was the head of the Catholic Church in England, which, before the Reformation of the sixteenth century, was the only recognized religious institution in England and Western Europe. But soon after becoming king, Henry II hired Becket away from the church to be his chancellor, or chief advisor. Although Becket was fifteen years older than Henry, the two men became close friends. They both enjoyed luxury and some of the more decadent enjoyments available to the wealthy and powerful aristocracy of medieval England.

The High Middle Ages was a period of developing tension between the pope in Rome and many of the secular rulers in far-off places such as England. In England, the church had its own government, with courts to try clerks and priests who broke the law. These courts and other state-like apparatus infuriated the hot-tempered Henry, who thought they diminished his power and authority.

Hoping to diffuse some of the church's power, Henry convinced a reluctant Becket to become the archbishop of Canterbury in 1162. Surely, his old friend would side with him on issues of church and state. But when Becket refused to agree with him that church officials who committed crimes, or so-called "criminous clerks," should be tried in royal and not church courts, a feud erupted between the two friends. As Becket refused to backdown to Henry's demands, the king grew angrier and angrier. Becket wisely fled to France. It was only after the pope intervened and brokered an agreement that Becket returned to England.

The pope's settlement was only a temporary truce. When the tensions between Henry and the church renewed, Becket excommunicated all church officials who sided with the king. On receiving this news, Henry flew into a rage and uttered the plea "to be free of this damned churchman." Four knights, wishing to curry favor with the king, hurried to Canterbury and murdered the archbishop in front of the main altar of the Cathedral.

Henry, who claimed that he had not meant for his utterance to be interpretted as an order, was full of remorse at the death of his old friend. To offer penance, he walked to Canterbury in sack cloth and ashes and asked the monks of the cathedral to flog him.

Soon after the martyrdom of Thomas Becket, claims were made of miracles occurring at the Cathedral. It became a shrine and a place of pilgrimage that many Christians visited at least once. The fourteenth-century poet Chaucer used the frame of a pilgrimage to Canterbury in his work *The Canterbury Tales*.

A thirteenth-century painting of Thomas Becket's murder.

four sons as eaglets bent on his destruction. Two of them had died in their prime: Geoffrey, the next-to-youngest son, tumbled to the ground in a tournament and galloping horses trampled him to death, and Young Henry perished while waging war against his father. Now Richard was a key player in the rebellion against him.

Abandoned not only by his son but many of his barons, Henry relied more and more on the counsel of the ever loyal William Marshal. As proof of his appreciation, the ailing king promised William one of the richest heiresses in England.

Now in his forties, William had waited a long time to find a rich wife who would provide him with land and wealth. When King Henry promised William eighteen-year-old Isabel of Striguil as his wife, William gave Heloise of Kendal to another man. Isabel, who had been living in the Tower of London since the death of her father thirteen years before, owned an impressive sixty-five-and-one-half fiefs.

In the Middle Ages, it was common for marriages to take place in order to form political and economic alliances. William himself was a product of such a marriage: His father had ended his first marriage by annulment to marry William's mother, Sybil, and thus end a feud with a neighbor. William's marriage to Isabel would secure his status as a landed baron.

The official marriage of William and Isabel, however, would have to wait. In the summer of 1189, Richard and King Philip launched a vigorous attack on King Henry at Le Mans. Forced to retreat, Henry ordered William to set fire to the town. As the flames spread, William encountered a woman struggling to remove furniture from her burning home. Overcome with compassion, William dismounted and rushed to help her. As he stooped down to pick up a smoldering eiderdown cover, flames licked his face. The smoke almost choked him before he could remove his helmet.

Soon the French set out in pursuit of the retreating English. William and a few of his men stayed behind to delay the chase, much as William's father had covered Mathilda's escape from the superior forces of King Stephen in 1141.

Euphoric over his victory, Richard made a nearly fatal mistake. Thinking his father's troops were routed, he threw off his gear. When William and his men appeared in ambush, Richard leaped on his horse and galloped off, wearing only one piece of armor: his iron helmet. William, fully armed, rode Richard down, pinning him with the point of his lance. "By the legs of God, Marshal, do not kill me," cried the prince, "that would not be right for I am unarmed."

Reluctantly, William agreed, "No, let the devil kill you for I shall not." Lowering his lance point, he killed Richard's horse, and Richard tumbled to the ground.

By this time, King Henry II was tired. Beaten and near death, the fifty-six-year-old monarch accepted the harsh terms of truce offered by the French. Then the weary king proceeded on to his fortress at Chinon. Henry's health grew worse daily. The news that his favorite son, John, had deserted from the army broke Henry's spirit. John was his only son who had remained loyal to him, even after his wife and other children had turned against him. This final heavy shame of John's desertion was too much for the king.

King Henry II died on July 6, 1189. One hundred years before, the servants of the king's court had abandoned William the Conqueror at the time of his death. Now, his descendant received similar treatment. Henry's servants plundered the royal chambers and stripped the clothing from his stiffening corpse before notifying his knights of their master's death.

The most powerful monarch of the twelfth century was dead, and the meinie had no royal robes of state for the body. When William attempted to scatter alms to the poor, he found the treasury empty. The poor howled in vain for the customary money.

William's last duty to his master was to follow the body to the abbey at Fontevrault. At the abbey, William apprehensively awaited the arrival of the future king. By his unswerving loyalty to King Henry, William had made an enemy of his son Richard.

Richard arrived at the abbey and stood impassively beside his father's corpse. No one could tell if he were "joyful, sad, remorseful, grieving or cheerful." After leaving the church, Richard summoned William Marshal. At first, the count teased William about trying to kill him on the road to Le Mans. "Sire, I had no intention of killing you, nor did I ever try to do so. I am still strong enough

This Old Testament miniature from the thirteenth century shows the death of a king in battle. The knights take his armor to a chapel and parade the king's head on a spear.

to direct my lance. If I had wished, I should have struck your body, as I did your horse. If I killed the horse, I did not do so by mistake, nor do I repent doing so." Richard then pardoned the outspoken knight. He admired William and had plans for him in his realm.

Some members of the late King Henry's household protested that William had been given the heiress of Striguil to marry. Richard claimed that his father had only promised to do so. As king, Richard could choose to give William the lady and her lands. Although Richard promised Isabel and all her lands to William, he kept a share of her inheritance for himself including Isabel's holdings in Ireland.

Following the funeral, William eagerly set out on his mission to England to marry Isabel. Riding at breakneck speed, he crossed Anjou, Maine, and Normandy, stopping along the way to take possessions of certain estates to which his wife-to-be was heir.

William arrived in England before the end of July. Following orders from Richard, he stopped at Winchester to deliver letters to the recently released Queen Eleanor, who had survived her enemy and husband. Seeing his patroness of long ago looking so well shocked William. During her fifteen years of captivity, Eleanor had managed to keep physically and mentally fit. After the king's death, the sixty-seven-year-old queen bounced back into action. She governed England until Richard could be crowned.

William left Winchester and headed to London and to Isabel. Word had reached Isabel that Henry II had promised her to William Marshal. After spending most of her life in safe keeping in the gloomy Tower of London, she was now marrying the most famous knight of the age, although he was more than twenty years her senior. Their marriage would last thirty years.

William arrived in London lacking the funds for the usual wedding festivities. He found it easy to borrow them, after all, he was soon to be a wealthy man. So, with appropriate pomp and ceremony, William married the heiress Isabel—"the good the fair, the wise, the courteous lady of high degree."

Only days before he had been worried for his life. Now he was William Marshal, Lord of Striguil, of Longueville, and of Leinster. Thirty-four years before he had journeyed from En-

gland to the court of Tancarville, the fourth son of a minor baron. A strong arm and a loyal heart had won him renown and riches.

Richard's return to England shortened the newlyweds' honeymoon. Preparations were well under way for the new king's coronation. In the days leading up to the spectacle, William stayed by the king's side.

Richard's coronation was the most magnificent pageant London had yet witnessed. Banners and tapestries decorated house fronts. The streets were swept clean and strewn with fresh

Richard I was crowned on September 13, 1189.

rushes for the procession that wound its way to Westminster Abbey on September 13, 1189.

Dignitaries carried the jeweled crown, the sword of state, and the coronation robes. Richard's brother John bore the massive golden spurs. The honor of carrying the royal scepter before the king in the processional went to William Marshal.

Queen Eleanor gazed with rapture at her son as he walked beneath a silk canopy held aloft by four barons. He wore the crusader's cross on his robe. His amber and gold hair fell to his shoulders, framing his handsome face. Tall and athletic, he had the air of a true king.

After being proclaimed Richard I, King of England, the new monarch stayed on English soil only long enough to raise money for the Third Crusade. Richard and Philip II of France prepared for a joint expedition to the Holy Land.

Every town, village, and port on both sides of the English Channel engaged in frenzied activity. Foresters felled huge oaks for shipbuilding. Black smoke belched from roaring forges as smiths hammered out horse-shoes, chain-mail, helmets, swords, and spears. The stench from the heated metal filled the air. Peasants slaughtered pigs, cured them, and stashed the hams on board ships. Never before had there been such elaborate preparations for a Crusade.

In March 1190, William Marshal and other barons met Richard in Normandy. William accompanied the king to Vézelay where the crusaders had assembled. Early in July, the two kings and their huge armies marched south to Marseilles and the waiting fleets. William headed to England and a new challenge.

Eleanor of Aquitaine was one of the most powerful and influential women of the Middle Ages. During her eighty-two-year life, her multiple reigns would span sixty-seven years and two countries. She died in 1204 and is buried in the abbey of Fontevrault beside her son Richard I.

CHAPTER SEVEN
THE MARSHAL

While King Richard I led the Third Crusade, William Marshal became a key player in running the king's business in England. His new position, however, placed William on a collision course with the king's brother John and the king's first chancellor, William Longchamp. These two men were enemies who began conniving for control of England as soon as Richard and the crusaders left for the East.

William faced a difficult predicament. As one of four justiciars (assistants) to the chancellor, he owed allegiance to Longchamp. But he could not afford to alienate John, who was a likely heir to the throne.

Early in 1191, King Richard, wintering in Sicily, received word of the problems involving Longchamp. The king issued a secret royal mandate authorizing William and the justiciars to replace the chancellor. In due time, the justiciars produced the royal document, thus ending the political duel. Longchamp fled to France dressed as a woman, and John remained powerful.

Meanwhile, Richard and Philip could not agree on how to conduct the Crusade. Before the end of 1191, Philip returned to

SALADIN

Saladin (1138-1193) was a Kurd born in present-day Iraq. Saladin, whose Arabic name was Salah al-Din Yusuf ibn Ayyub, went to Egypt at age fourteen to help fight the European crusaders. Saladin's uncle was the Kurdish commander. When his uncle died in 1169, Saladin became the commander of the army and a chief minister to the Egyptian rulers.

Middle Eastern politics was treacherous, but Saladin knew that before the crusaders could be ejected from the Holy Land he needed to organize the warring Arabs into a unified force. It took seventeen years for the brilliant military strategists to gain control of Egypt and Syria.

Saladin fought Richard the Lion Heart for control of Jerusalem.

The Europeans had captured the Holy City of Jerusalem in 1099. Upon seizing the city, they had massacred its Muslim and Jewish citizens and then divided the area around the Holy City into four military areas. In 1186, Saladin began a campaign to recapture Jerusalem. Over a period of months he defeated the Christians and recaptured the city in October 1187.

The Europeans launched the Third Crusade under the leadership of Richard the Lion Heart and King Philip II of France. Although Richard bested Saladin in several battles, he could never retake the city. In 1192, Saladin and Richard made a treaty that allowed for Arab control of Jerusalem. Saladin died the next year.

France. He grew tired of the overbearing conduct of the English king and the hot, dusty desert with its mosquitoes, tarantulas, and nauseating flies.

King Richard continued the holy war without him for another year and a half. When the Muslims failed to keep their promises after an assault on Acre (now Akko, Israel) King Richard ordered 3,000 prisoners butchered in front of their countrymen. This act of defiance earned him the name "Lion Heart."

Not long afterwards, Richard received letters from Eleanor alerting him that he was in danger of losing his kingdom to John. Richard impulsively abandoned all hope of seizing Jerusalem and made a three-year truce with Saladin, the renowned Muslim warrior and leader. In October 1192, King Richard left the Holy Land, ending the Third Crusade. On his way home, disaster struck when Richard's ship wrecked. He survived but was captured and imprisoned in Germany.

With his brother imprisoned in a foreign land, a gleeful John plotted with Philip of France to seize the English crown. His plans were ended prematurely when the Germans agreed to release Richard. Eleanor—who had so recently been a prisoner herself—cringed at the thought of her son languishing in a remote cell. She set out to raise the ransom by taxing every person and institution that she could. A year later, she set sail across the English Channel with chests bulging with silver. After Richard gained his freedom, the aging queen fell weeping into her son's arms.

When John heard that his brother was free and on his way back to England, he feared for his life. He hurried to France, hoping for help from King Philip. But the French king turned his back on him.

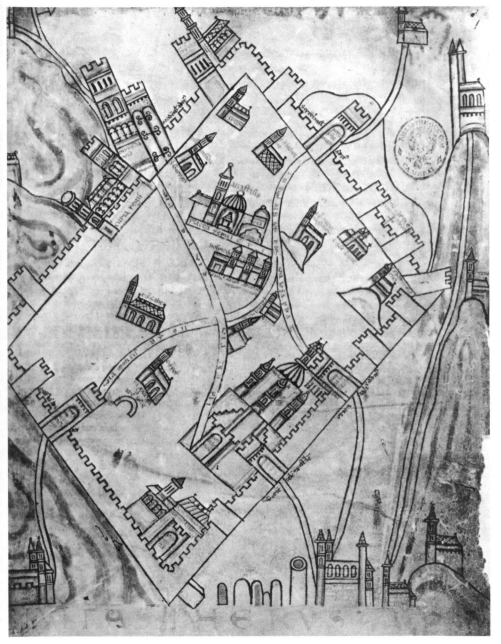

A twelfth-century map of the city of Jerusalem.

Richard the Lion Heart returned to England in the spring of 1194—four years and three months since the day he had left. A hero's welcome of feasts and lavish gifts awaited him. The fact that he had deserted his subjects, taxed them to pay for his Crusade, and even offered to sell London to fund the Holy Wars was soon forgotten.

William was at Striguil Castle (known as Chepstow Castle today) when he heard the news of Richard's landing at Sandwich. At the same time, a messenger informed him that his elder brother, John Marshal, was dead. Torn between going to meet his king or attending to the burial of his brother, he exclaimed: "Although I have never been so afflicted as by the death of my brother, the coming of my lord has brought the best of consolations. I thank God as much for the adversity as for the prosperity which has come on me so fast, because such joy have I in the king's coming that I can stand against the grief I did not believe I could face."

William acted judiciously. He sent knights from his retinue to escort his brother's body. On his way to meet the king, he stopped at Cirencester to view the body and comfort his brother's widow. After mass, he sent his brother's corpse and widow onto Bradenstoke priory for the burial. Whatever grief William felt for his brother did not keep him from joining the king.

With Richard in control of England again, there was no more need for William to serve as a justiciar, and he replaced one role with another. His brother's death left William the inheritor to the Marshal family lands and the title of marshal to the king's court. At this time, he became commonly known as "the Marshal." He wasted no time performing the duties necessary to protect the king. At Nottingham, the last of John's castles, the Marshal assisted Richard in reducing the remnant of John's supporters.

Following the surrender at Nottingham, Richard thanked the men who had worked under severe handicaps to carry on the government during the Crusade. He singled out the Marshal for serving honorably in his absence. The Marshal replied, "Sire, we have only done our duty. For his lord a right-minded man ought to suffer willingly every kind of hardship and distress."

Richard's party stopped for the night at the royal hunting preserve in Sherwood Forest. Later ballads told the story of how Richard met the famous outlaw Robin Hood. Disguised as an abbot, Richard rode into the dark forest where he found the good-hearted outlaw who robbed the rich to pay the poor. The strange abbot drilled Robin Hood with questions to find out which monarch he supported: King Richard or his conniving brother, John. Satisfied with Robin Hood's answers, the abbot chucked his disguise, and King Richard joined the merry men in a great feast under the greenwood tree.

After reaching a truce with his brother John, Richard did not linger in his homeland. (He spent only a total of six months of his ten-year reign in England.) The warrior king headed for Normandy to recapture the lands and castles taken from him by King Philip. The Marshal joined Richard there in May 1194. Even with all his wealth and power, the Marshal still loved fighting. He welcomed the opportunity to lead troops in battle again. But this time, he too had a stake in Normandy: his lands at Longueville.

Except for brief visits to England and Wales to check on his estates, the Marshal spent the next five years in France where his growing family made their home in Normandy. Isabel gave birth to their first son, William, in 1190. She bore more children, almost one a year, until they had five sons and five daughters. These years were successful for the Marshal on the battlefield, as well. The English scored ongoing victories over the French, raising the Marshal's already high favor in the English court.

The war between Richard and Philip dragged on year after year, interspersed by short periods of truce. To protect the northern borders of Normandy, William designed and built a castle on a rocky summit overlooking the Seine River. With its round towers, Château Gaillard represented an advancement in castle architecture. While traveling in the East, the Marshal had noted that round towers were more easily defensible than the square towers popular in England and France.

In May 1197, the English forces stormed the French castle of Milly-sur-Thérain. Richard's army scaled up ladders set against the walls, but the garrison fought back vigorously using stakes, arrows, forks, and flails. The defenders knocked down the crowded ladders, hurling besiegers into the ditch. Standing on the edge of the moat, the Marshal directed the assault.

As the attackers began to fall back, one knight was left clinging to a ladder, a pitchfork caught around his neck. Seeing the knight's predicament, the Marshal leaped fully armed into the moat, climbed up the opposite bank, and clambered up the ladder with a drawn sword. Swinging left and right, he rescued the knight and defended a section of the wall as other besiegers rushed to assist. He flattened the constable of the castle with one mighty blow to his helmet. Then he sat down on his unconscious captive and watched while the English took the castle.

After the fight, the Marshal received a mild rebuke from Richard: "It is not fitting for a man of your rank and prowess to risk yourself in such feats. Leave them to young knights who must win renown," the king reprimanded him.

The Marshal's duties included more than leading military exploits. Just as he had served as a wise counselor to Henry II and the Young King, he also counseled King Richard. He advised the hot-tempered Richard both in military matters and affairs of state. On a number of occasions, the Marshal's tact and diplomatic skills averted serious conflict between Richard and the Church.

Such was the Marshal's influence that he once dared to approach Richard after he had shut himself in his room, raging and screaming about Philip's proposed terms for peace. The Marshal scolded the king for being angry without cause: "Sire, you ought to have been laughing for you have gained everything." After soothing Richard's temper, the Marshal assured him of the advantageous terms. In March 1199, the two kings signed a five-year truce. One month later, however, this peaceful state of affairs ended abruptly.

There was an old ballad whose verses warned that King Richard would die by an arrow made in Limoges. While the Marshal attended to royal business in Normandy, King Richard marched south to Limoges to settle a minor dispute with a vassal. He stormed the vassal's small castle, declaring to hang the defenders from the battlements.

From his post upon the ramparts, one of the defenders spotted the king. Remembering the ballad, he fitted an arrow into his bow and let it fly. The arrow struck Richard down, penetrating under his left shoulder blade. Richard's men fought on, the castle was taken, and every one of the defenders was hanged. Meanwhile, Richard lay on his sick bed in agonizing pain, the barb wound festering. Eleven days later on April 6, 1199, the king died.

Before his death, Richard had sent sealed letters to the

Marshal informing him of his serious injury and ordering him to take command of the castle and treasury at Rouen. Without delay, the Marshal and the Archbishop of Canterbury rode to Rouen. Four days later, a second envoy arrived, bearing the news that King Richard was now dead.

The Marshal had just pulled off his boots when the messenger reported the news. Despite the late hour, the Marshal dressed and hastened to consult with the archbishop regarding succession.

Richard died without a son to follow him onto the throne. The two possible heirs were his brother John and his twelve-year-old nephew, Arthur. The archbishop favored Arthur of Brittany, son of Henry II's deceased son Geoffrey. But the Marshal had

committed himself to John's side many years before. After hours of debate, the archbishop begrudgingly conceded, predicting that the Marshal would live to regret this decision.

Though the Marshal supported John's claims to the throne, he was fully aware of the new king's weaknesses. The Marshal soothed the disgruntled English barons, who remembered how John had tried to seize the throne during Richard's captivity. But the Marshal's support carried the day, and the barons reluctantly went along

John was named King of England after Richard's sudden death.

with his decision. The new king wisely rewarded the Marshal for his services in securing the kingdom for him with gifts of land and castles.

CHAPTER EIGHT

FEUDAL LORD

On May 27, 1199, the same day of John's coronation, the thirty-two-year-old king granted William Marshal the title of Earl of Pembroke. Pembroke, in southwest England, had been a possession of Isabel's family for generations. Its location provided a staging ground for invasions of Ireland. With the granting of the land, William Marshal, Earl of Pembroke, reached a zenith of wealth and prestige.

The Marshal first visited Ireland—a short crossing from Pembroke Castle—in 1201 with Isabel. Before reaching the Irish shore, a ferocious storm struck. Mountainous waves cascaded over the bow of the ship causing it to buck like a giant seesaw for "a day and a night."

The threat of drowning in the Irish Sea at the height of his fortunes seemed a cruel joke to the Marshal. He bargained with God, vowing that if he survived the raging storm, he would build an abbey in Ireland. Safe on Irish soil, he promptly began construction on Tintern Parva Abbey, or "Little Tintern," modeled after the Welsh Tintern Abbey. Founding a religious house was a mark of prestige for an aristocrat in medieval Europe. This was not the first time that the Marshal had built a house of God. Shortly after his marriage to Isabel, he acknowledged God's grace for his good fortune by establishing a priory at Cartmel.

When the Marshal returned to London, King John lavished him with gifts, including the castles of Gloucester and Bristol. Between May 1199 and the end of 1201, the Marshal reached the height of his career as court favorite. He successfully defended the northern borders of Normandy against King Philip of France who had refused to acknowledge John as king of England. But in 1203, King John's continental domains began to fall apart.

During this period, John's nephew, young Arthur, had continued to gather support from those who opposed his uncle. John took Arthur prisoner in Rouen. When Arthur disappeared, the rumor quickly spread that King John had stabbed his nephew to death and thrown his body in the Seine. John was an obsessively suspicious, even paranoid, king. His defeats and loss of land in France, along with his unpleasant nature, had already undercut his subjects' trust. The alleged murder of Arthur put more strain on his relationship with the barons.

The Marshal continued to serve his king on the battlefield. In the latter part of 1203, William led a large force under cover of night to try to reclaim the fortress of Château Gaillard. But the expedition failed, and the Marshal and King John sailed for England. By December 1203, the vast majority of Normandy—the original holdings of the Plantagenet family—was lost.

The following spring, King John sent the Marshal as part of an embassy to the French court. The peace mission failed, but the Marshal used the opportunity to negotiate with King Philip to retain control of his Norman lands. Philip demanded that if

The interior of Tintern Abbey, Wales. William Marshal based the design of Tintern Parva, or "Little Tintern," on this larger abbey.

the Marshal wanted to keep his land, he make an exclusive liege homage to the French king. A liege homage meant that the Marshal had to swear not to engage in battle against the French; if he did so he would forfeit his land. William asked for time to consider, and Philip, in return for a substantial sum of money, agreed to give him a year to decide. The fact that the Marshal eventually agreed to Philip's demand is evidence of his weakening confidence in the English king. He was willing to risk King John's displeasure and the possibility of disgrace. Today, the written terms of the 1204 liege homage survive in Paris.

The Marshal returned to England and an angry King John. This was not the first time he had disputed with John. In 1203, Marshal had bravely told his master that it was his own fault that he had no friends. Boldly, he pointed out that John had alienated his followers.

King John gave the Marshal verbal permission to do homage to Philip and sent letters to the same effect to the French court. But when William next returned from France, King John reproached him: "Marshal, I know for certain that you have done homage and sworn fealty and allegiance against me and to my hurt."

The Marshal replied, "Sire, you know well that I have done nothing against you and what I did was done with your permission."

"That is not true," responded the king.

In June, the king summoned the Marshal and the other magnates to accompany him on an expedition to recover Poitou. To do so would break the terms of his homage, and the Marshal refused. Both men appealed to the judgment of the barons to settle their dispute, but their request for mediation was rejected.

The barons wisely preferred not to get involved. The heated argument ended when the Marshal willingly handed over his eldest son—by then fifteen years of age—to the king as a hostage for his good behavior. For the first time in his career as a magnate, the Marshal found himself out of royal favor.

The Marshal coped with the mental strain by getting away, much as he had in 1182 immediately following his breach with Young Henry. He sought King John's permission to visit his lands in Ireland. King John, continuing to treat the Marshal with suspicion, initially refused him. Only after relinquishing his second son, Richard, as a hostage was the Marshal given permission to go. Early in 1207, William arrived in Ireland with his wife and meinie.

In September, the king ordered the Marshal to return to England. Before his departure, William held council with his men and his wife. Isabel, who was pregnant, distrusted John and wondered why he had requested her husband to return to England. She had not wanted her son Richard given over to the king as a hostage. Now she would be left alone to defend their interests in Ireland.

The Marshal felt he had no choice but to do as his master asked. He made a final address to his men of Leinster: "Lords! See the countess, whom I here present to you; your lady by

William Marshal swore leige homage to King Philip II of France to keep his lands in Normandy.

WILLIAM MARSHAL

birth, the daughter of the earl who . . . conquered this land. She remains amongst you pregnant. Until God permits me to return, I pray you to keep her well and faithfully, for she is your lady, and I have nothing but through her."

The Marshal received a cold welcome on his return to the English court. Clearly, King John had come to fear him. Over time, however, as William convinced John that he was no threat to his rule, the king softened his attitude and allowed the Marshal to return to Ireland for the next four years.

In 1213, the threat of a French invasion forced King John to summon the Marshal back to England. John also freed the Marshal's sons, who had been held hostage all these years. With his customary allegiance, the Marshal returned to the royal court. "He took no heed of what had gone before with the king, nor his cruelty, because ever he loved loyalty."

King John made another attempt to reclaim Normandy in July 1214, but suffered defeat. This time he returned to England to face the rebellion of his barons. He had pitilessly taxed his citizens to pay for his failed military expeditions, and his other repressive policies had incurred hostility also. Many barons refused to meet payments they owed the king.

Serving as chief negotiator for King John, the Marshal met with the disgruntled barons and listened to their demands, which he brought back to the king. But John refused to negotiate. Instead, he demanded total subservience. Enraged, the barons formed an army and seized London. Soon it was obvious John did not have a chance in the face of the mass resistance. He dispatched William Marshal "for the sake of peace" to the barons with a message that he would grant their demands.

On June 15, 1215, King John met the barons at Runnymede—

a pleasant meadow by the Thames—and signed the Magna Carta. This document limited the king's power, provided a new system of courts, and promised that no Englishman could be put in prison without a trial. William Marshal signed his name as a witness to the charter.

Following the signing, John immediately broke the terms of the Magna Carta and returned to the battlefield against the barons. While John marched about England, ravaging the lands of his rebellious barons in the east and torching the north, the Marshal organized resistance to the Welsh, who had also risen up against English control in the west. The Marshal was in an uncomfortable situation during this period. His sense of loyalty compelled him to support his lord, yet his sense of justice prevented him from agreeing with John's policies.

The barons, seeking French support for their rebellion, offered the English crown to Louis, son of King Philip. King John sent the Marshal to the French court. For the last time, the Marshal crossed the English Channel to France and appealed to Philip to forbid his son to invade England. But his pleas fell on deaf ears. The chance to make trouble for his nemesis King John was irresistable to Philip.

When Louis of France arrived in England two months later with his forces, the Marshal's namesake, younger William Marshal, was one of the first to make homage to the French prince. At first glance, this appeared to show a split in the Marshal's family with the father supporting King John and the son backing Prince Louis. But rumors soon circulated that the Marshal had encouraged his son to side with the barons and act as an informant in case King John lost the struggle or caved beneath the pressure.

After several months of fighting on English soil, John fell ill. The now penitent king cried out on his deathbed, "Pray the Marshal to pardon the wrongs I have done him . . . and since I am more sure of his loyalty than that of any other man, I pray you give him the care of my son." Then King John, the last of Henry II's troubled sons and one of the most detested of English kings, died.

William Marshal had outlived another master. He was now an old man, and he wished to live out his days in tranquility. But the Marshal had made himself indispensable to the English royalty, and his last years were to be the busiest of his long life.

CHAPTER NINE

PROTECTOR OF ENGLAND

Following King John's burial, the royal court was thrown into chaos. The king's heir, his nine-year-old son, Henry Plantagenet, had been kept safe during the rebellion at the castle of Devizes. Prince Louis of France now lay claim to half of the English kingdom. The treasury was empty, depleted by years of senseless wars. Members of the royalist party, those who had supported King John, assembled at Gloucester to solve the dilemma. First, they sent for the young Henry Plantagenet to be brought to the court. The Marshal rode out to meet the heavily armed royal party on the road to Gloucester.

When Henry's party approached, the Marshal saluted the boy-heir. Young Henry knew and liked William Marshal. When he saw him he called out a greeting and then asked God to give the Marshal the power to protect him. "Sire," replied the Marshal, "by my soul I shall do what I can to serve you in good faith and with all my powers." The boy wept. Everyone present shed tears, including the Marshal, as they turned their horses toward Gloucester.

Fearing that Louis might use the confusion surrounding

John's death to grab the English throne, the council decided to knight and anoint the young lad at once. There was little question who should knight the young prince: "Who other, even if there were a thousand of us, would be the most qualified by his ability than William the Marshal . . . I assert that he must gird on this boy's sword." The Marshal had already knighted one king. Now the honor of dubbing another king a knight went to him as well.

Following the ritual, Henry—dressed in royal robes hastily cut down to his size—was crowned King Henry III on October 28, 1216, in the abbey at Gloucester. Only ten days after King John's death, the royalists had a new king. There remained one large problem. Although a nine-year-old king could reign, he could not rule. Until Henry III came of age, the kingdom needed a strong hand to restore order. After discussion, the nobles agreed to abide by their late king's wish. They offered the guardianship of Henry III, and therefore of England, to William Marshal. He was asked to serve as Regent of England until the young king reached maturity.

As a lord and a war hero, the Marshal already had power and prestige. Under the late King Richard, he had gained administrative experience in handling the affairs of government. His activities on the continent as knight, warrior, and diplomat made him well known in the French court. Because of his wisdom and discretion, four kings had sought his counsel. Both friends and enemies admired his reputation for honesty and loyalty. His personality and experience made him more than suitable for the eminent office. But William Marshal initially wanted to reject the offer. He insisted that he was too old (exaggerating his age by ten years) and too feeble to be regent.

The royalist council insisted. The Marshal consulted his

nephew John Marshal (bastard son of his brother John), his squire John of Earley, and Sheriff Ralph Musard about undertaking this enormous responsibility. The Marshal's nephew urged him to accept. Seeing the promise of great riches for the Marshal's men, the sheriff agreed. But the Marshal's faithful squire advised him to refuse because of his age and the poor economic conditions of the country. In view of the conflicting opinions, the Marshal decided to sleep on the matter.

When the council of nobles reconvened the next day, the Marshal reiterated his misgivings, which were speedily dismissed. He summoned his three friends, telling them that he was on the brink of a "sea without bottom or bank." John of Earley, now less discouraging, pointed out the honor to be gained in so difficult a position.

A flood of memories swept over the Marshal, harking to the time when he, even younger than little Henry, had been abandoned and sentenced to death. Turning to his faithful squire, he said, "Your advice is true and good. If everyone abandons the boy but me, do you know what I shall do? I will carry him on my back, and if I can hold him up, I will hop from island to island, from country to country, even if I have to beg for my bread."

And so, the Marshal began what was to be his last and greatest adventure. As regent, the Marshal exercised the power and authority of a king. Within days of the coronation, the Marshal used his seal on letters and grants issued in the king's name.

William Marshal's first task was to end the internal conflict in England that had festered and erupted over the sixteen years of growing discontent under John's rule. He needed to take steps to retain the loyalty of the royalist barons and to win back the rebellious ones. The job was made more difficult because it had no precedent. No king of England had come to the throne as a minor since the days of the Norman Conquest.

With the royal treasury empty and the late king's mercenaries clamoring for unpaid wages, the Marshal devised creative ways of raising money to run the government and to drive Louis out of England. He dipped into the reserve fund of the English crown. Jewels and rich garments stored in royal castles at Devizes and Corfe were sold or traded. He sent constables out with rings set with precious stones—emeralds, sapphires, diamonds, garnets, and rubies—to purchase supplies. Captains of mercenary troops received jewelry and other valuables to pay their men. Silk garments became payments on money fiefs. The Marshal had no qualms about selling the royal treasure to assist the country in time of dire need.

On November 11, 1216, the royalists issued a revised version of the Magna Carta in the name of Henry III. The new charter omitted certain phrases contained in the original. Changes relating to taxation and safeguards of national liberties reflected the Marshal's wisdom and ability. This document, bearing the Marshal's seal, promised that the new king's government would renounce John's errors.

During the winter of 1217, lack of resources had prevented the Marshal from taking action against Louis. In February, the Marshal launched his first serious campaign against the French prince. His plan was to cut Louis off from the sea, preventing him from returning to France for reinforcements. Louis realized Marshal's strategy and, by the time the regent and the royal army reached the coast, Louis had already sailed. Marshal then set out to reclaim important castles, disrupt French communications, and cut off any supplies before Louis returned.

When Louis returned to England in April, he found many of his followers had joined the royalists in his absence. Those loyal to Henry had regained castles in the south of England.

Louis decided to divide his army. Part of the rebel forces marched toward Lincoln Castle, long under siege but still held for the royalists under the command of the defiant Nicola de la Haie. Louis marched with the remainder of his army to besiege Dover Castle. The Marshal seized the opportunity presented by Louis splitting his forces to mount a vigorous attack on the French at Lincoln Castle. On May 19, 1217, the Marshal's modest army of 406 knights and 317 crossbow men left Newark for Lincoln.

On the twenty-five mile journey, the Marshal's men marched joyfully as if to a tournament. Still ringing in their ears were the words of the Marshal's pre-battle address:

"Listen to me, all you loyal knights . . . We are fighting for our honour, ourselves, and our loved ones, our wives, our children and our land; we are fighting for the peace of Holy Church . . . and the pardon of our sins. Let us therefore accept this great honour and bear the brunt of battle, and let there not be a coward amongst us."

Medieval warfare was bloody and strenuous. These chain-mail clad knights battle on horseback and foot.

Early the following morning, the royalist army reached the city, their horses exhausted by the swift pace. The Marshal expected to battle the French in an open field, but deceived by the size of the advancing host (each English baron carried two banners, one with his troops and another with his baggage) the enemy retired inside the walls and closed the gates.

Dame Nicola sent word to the Marshal that his troops could enter through a back gate. Finding the unguarded gate, the Marshal's army stampeded into the castle. Stiff-jointed as he was, the Marshal spurred his horse forward, dashing into the ranks of the enemy "as swift as a bird and as fierce as a hungry lion." Fifty years earlier, the young William Marshal had charged headlong into his first battle at Drincourt. The old tourney, *"Dieu aide au Marchal!"*, rang out again, and the brisk battle took on the appearance of a tournament. The English, although far outnumbered by the French, carried the day. The French and their English supporters fled the castle. This would be the Marshal's last battle.

The French defeat at Lincoln was not enough, however, to persuade Louis to leave England. The French prince, headquartered in London, awaited reinforcements from across the Channel. Rumors reached the Marshal that a great army mustered by Blanche of Castille, wife of Louis, was set to sail for England. Weary but undeterred, the Marshal and his followers headed for the coast, where he had ordered the mariners to assemble their ships at Sandwich.

On the morning of August 24, 1217, William Marshal ordered his twenty-two ships—some large, some small but all well equipped with arms and men—to sail out to meet the approaching gigantic French fleet.

Because his men had persuaded him that his life was too valuable to risk in a hazardous sea battle, the Marshal stayed ashore. On that clear morning, the regent and the boy-king watched the naval fight from the cliffs.

The French flagship, carrying supplies and troops to reinforce Louis, sailed forward to attack. The ship, overloaded with a special siege machine and magnificent horses, rode low in the water, its sides almost submerged. In contrast, the flat-bottomed boats of the English skimmed the high waves. When they approached close enough, the English defenders hurled potfuls of lye from the top of the swells into the eyes of the enemy below.

Then, leaping onto the French ship, the English captured all the Frenchmen, including the captain and master, Eustace the monk, who was given the choice of having his head cut off on the siege machine or over the side of the vessel. Whichever method he chose, his head soon floated in the water.

The sea battle of Sandwich was a decisive victory for the English. Louis realized that the destruction of his reinforcements meant the end of his hopes of conquering England. The terms of the peace negotiations called for the withdrawal of the French. In addition, the regency paid Louis a large sum for his losses and expenses in exchange for a promise to restore the land in France that King John had lost back to Henry III. Although he agreed to these terms, Louis never fulfilled his promises.

Peace finally restored, William Marshal led England in the slow recovery from civil warfare over the next nineteen months. He reinstated the rebel barons in their lands, released war prisoners, and collected money for the payment to Louis. The war had left many of the Marshal's own lands and castles ravaged. In 1217, he acquired his childhood home at Marlborough after it was reclaimed from the French. He also took possession of Newbury Castle, where he was nearly hanged by King Stephen more than sixty years before.

The Marshal and his council reorganized the administrative system and worked to better systemize the king's finances. They reorganized the judicial system and once again the king's justices rode their circuits throughout the counties of England.

As the second year of his reign as regent drew to a close, the Marshal had reason to feel proud of his accomplishments. Faced with a barren treasury, hostile barons, and a foreign invader, he had raised money, won over many of the rebels, and defeated Louis. Now England was at peace.

CHAPTER TEN
FACING DEATH

The two years he struggled with the almost overwhelming burdens of government had sapped the old man's strength. William Marshal, who had started out life the penniless and landless younger son of a minor lord, had attained the highest honor his country had to offer. His extraordinary elevation and survival in a tumultuous era were due to his prowess, generosity, wisdom, and loyalty. But the time had come for him to step off the stage. Three years earlier, he had protested that he was too old, too weak, too out of joint to be regent. But he had risen to the task and had thankfully remained in robust health, until a sudden illness struck near the end of January 1219.

Although he made a slight recovery, the seventy-two-year-old knight realized the end was near. Unable to mount a horse, he ordered his men to row him upriver from London to Caversham on the Thames, his favorite English home. There, though racked with pain, he continued to transact business from his deathbed. Most of all, the young king's future troubled the Marshal. He wrestled with the question of whom to pass on the duty of regency and guardianship.

After deliberating with his barons, the Marshal saw no one capable of taking his place as regent. To avert certain calamity for the country, he chose to place twelve-year-old Henry III in the care of the papal legate, the pope's representative at the English court.

The Marshal took the young king's hand in his and said, "Sire, I pray the Lord God . . . would grant my prayer that you should become an honorable man; but that if it should be otherwise and you follow the example of some wicked ancestor, then I pray God . . . will not grant you a long life, but that you may die young." With this veiled criticism of Henry's father, King John, the Marshal relinquished his role as regent of England.

The Marshal lingered for another month at Caversham, refusing all food except bread-stuffed mushrooms. He released his private possessions and provided for the division of his holdings in four countries. According to custom, Countess Isabel's vast inheritance would return to her. William, the eldest son, would inherit the ancestral Marshal lands. And after his mother's death, he would inherit her fiefs, as well.

All of his sons but the youngest received an inheritance. The dying man then turned to his knights. "Lords, one of my sons, Anselm, has received nothing even though he is very dear to me. If he lives to become a knight and shows merit, he will find, even though he has no land, someone who will love and honor him above all men."

John of Earley felt sorry for the landless lad. "Ah, Lord, do not do that. Give him at least enough money to buy shoes for his horses." The Marshal gave in and granted his youngest son land in Ireland worth 140 pounds.

The Marshal had arranged distinguished marriages for four

of his five daughters. He was concerned over his unmarried daughter, Jeanne. "If only she too were well married my soul would be more at ease . . . I will that she have thirty acres of land and 200 marks to go on with until such time as God takes care of her."

The day he sealed his will (one of the few surviving texts of baronial testaments before the late thirteenth century) the Marshal made a confession to his family and vassals. He told them that he had made a commitment while in the Holy Land to die in the Templar order. This meant he had to turn away from the world and take the habit as a monk. He waited until the onset of death, as did many Templars, before taking the habit. After kissing Isabel for the last time, the aging knight became a monk. Secretly, a year before, the Marshal had made a white cloak decorated with a red cross which was spread over him. He was too weak to put it on properly.

Then the Marshal asked John of Earley to hurry to Wales and bring back two silken shrouds he had stored in one of his castles. When the squire returned to the death chamber, he gave his master the slightly faded shrouds. The Marshal asked that they be displayed for all to see. "Lords, look here. I have had these cloths for thirty years. I bore them with me when I returned from the Holy Land so that they might be laid over my body when it is buried."

As the Marshal grew weaker, the death chamber never emptied. The public crowded in to visit him as he lay dying. On one occasion, he called John of Earley to his side. "I do not know why it is, but for the last three years I have never had such a strong desire to sing as during these last three days." The squire thought singing might bring back his appetite. "It would not do me any good, and everyone would believe me to be crazy," replied the Marshal.

Instead, his five daughters came forward to sing for him. When Jeanne's voice cracked with grief, the Marshal instructed her on how to sing the words clearly. After the girls finished singing, the Marshal dismissed them.

Then the Marshal called his eldest son and told him to remain beside him to the end and to accompany his body to London. He instructed him to feed and clothe at least a hundred poor folk after the ceremony.

On the day before he died, the Marshal's faithful squire asked him what he wanted done with his many robes and furs that were stashed in his wardrobe. A clerk suggested that the collection of rich clothing be sold and the money used to buy prayers for the Marshal's redemption. "Say no more wretches. I have had enough of your advice. Soon it will be Pentecost, the season when the knights of my house are to receive their new gowns." He ordered the distribution of the robes to his knights.

At noon the following day, family, church officials, and knights crowded the chamber. Its windows and doors were flung open. While an attendant rinsed his face with rose water, the Marshal said farewell to his family. "I am dying. I commend you to God. I can no longer remain with you. I cannot defend myself from death." Then William Marshal died in his son's arms with his eyes fixed on a cross. It was May 14, 1219.

The Marshal's body was set in state at the abbey of Reading. That night, the knights stood vigil, just as the Marshal watched over the bodies of his masters. The next day, the funeral procession made its way toward London with the sort of pomp usually reserved for royalty. The many nobles and their retinues who had

joined the cortège formed a guard of honor around the Marshal's remains.

After mass at Westminster Abbey, the Archbishop of Canterbury performed the burial service in the Temple Church. He stated that William Marshal had been "the best knight in the world." The ceremony concluded with the distribution of money and food to the dense mob of poor people who had awaited the death for three months. People said the Marshal fed the poor better than a king.

The Marshal's enemy on the battlefield, King Philip of France, offered a tribute: "William Marshal was, in my judgment, the most loyal man and true I have ever known, in any country I have been." One of the French knights, a valiant rival, proclaimed, "Sire, I judge that this was the wisest knight that was ever seen, in any land, in our age."

The effigy of William Marshal, medieval England's greatest knight, at Temple Church, London.

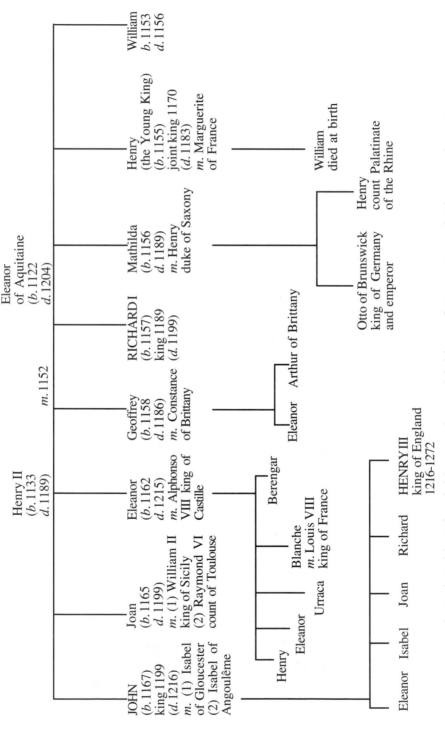

Genealogical Table: The children and grandchildren of Henry II and Eleanor of Aquitaine.

Glossary

abbot: The head of an abbey of monks.

archbishop: The chief bishop, or priest, of a province.

banneret: A knight entitled to bring vassals onto the field under his own banner.

bard: Armor used for the protection of a knight's horse.

baron: A member of the lowest order of English nobility. The title is given by the king in exchange for service and loyalty.

basinet: A helmet fitted with a visor.

catapult: A military machine worked by levers for throwing stones, darts, etc.

chain-mail armor: Made of small, metal rings that were linked together, chain-mail was the earliest type of armor.

chamberlain: A personal attendant of a king or nobleman.

chivalry: The code of behavior for medieval knights that stressed honor and loyalty.

colée: The traditional dubbing of a knight on the shoulder or head.

courtly love: The code of behavior for members of royal courts originating in the Poitiers court of Eleanor of Aquitaine that stressed respect for women, good behavior, and loyalty.

crupper: A strap that prevents the saddle from slipping forward on a horse.

Crusade: Any of the numerous wars in the eleventh, twelfth, and thirteenth centuries to recover Jerusalem and the Holy Lands from the Muslims.

feudalism: The system of social organization in the Middle Ages in which land was granted by the king to his vassals in exchange for homage and military service.

fief: An area of land, including villages or a manor, that a king awarded his vassal.

flail: A studded metal ball attached to a wooden handle by a chain for use as a weapon.

hauberk: A piece of chain-mail designed to protect the head and shoulders. Later, the hauberk was extended to cover the torso as a long tunic.

herald: An official who represented rulers or knights at war and at tournaments. Heralds also made certain that the rules of *heraldry* were maintained.

heraldry: The practice of carrying a *coat of arms* into battle or at a tournament in order to identify oneself. A coat of arms is a symbol used to represent a lord. Strict rules were created around the practice of heraldry regarding the types of symbols that could be used.

justiciar: The administrators of the Norman and early Plantagenet kings who presided over the king's court.

lance: A spear with a long wooden shaft and an iron or steel head.

Magna Carta: The document first signed by King John in 1213 that limited the king's power.

meinie: A military household.

melee: A battle involving many people in close proximity.

mercenaries: Knights who were paid to fight.

magnate: A great or noble person.

minstrel: A medieval entertainer who sang, played music, recited poetry, and danced.

palisade: A fence made of strong, pointed stakes.

Plantagenet: Any of the kings of England from Henry II to Richard III. The name comes from the habit of Henry II wearing a sprig of broom, or *planta genista*, in his cap.

plate armor: A type of armor made of metal plates that covered the body better than chain-mail.

quintain: An object mounted on a post that is used as a target for practicing the joust.

regent: A person invested with royal authority on behalf of another.

royalist: English noblemen who supported King John during the Third Crusade, and later, Prince Louis of France.

shroud: A sheet in which a corpse is wrapped for burial.

siege machine: A machine of war, such as the catapult.

squire: A young man in training to be a knight who acted as a knight's attendant.

tilting: To engage in a joust or similar contest.

tournament: A meeting where knights engaged in mock battle. Earlier tournaments featured more players on larger fields, while later tournaments took place in a more orderly fashion with one-on-one combat in a small arena.

troubadour: A medieval lyrical poet who composed and sang verses on the themes of chivalry and courtly love.

usury: To lend money in exchange for payment plus interest.

Bibliography

Barber, Richard. *The Knight and Chivalry, Revised Ed.* Suffolk, UK: The Boydell Press, 1995.

Barlow, Frank. *The Feudal Kingdom of England 1042-1216, Fifth Edition.* New York: Longman, 1999.

Coss, Peter. *The Knight in Medieval England 1000-1400.* Conshohocken, PA: Combined Books, Inc., 1993.

Crosland, Jessie. *William the Marshal.* London: Peter Owen LTD, 1962.

Crouch, David. *William Marshal: Court, Career and Chivalry in the Angevin Empire 1147-1219.* London: Longman, 1994.

Duby, Georges. *William Marshal: The Flower of Chivalry.* New York: Pantheon Books, 1986.

Gies, Frances. *The Knight in History.* New York: Harper & Row, 1984.

Gies, Joseph & Frances. *Life in a Medieval Castle.* New York: Harper & Row, 1974.

Gillingham, John. *Richard Coeur De Lion*. London: The Hambledon Press, 1994.

———."War and Chivalry in the History of William the Marshal," *Thirteen Century England II*. Edited by P. R. Coss and S. D. Lloyd. Suffolk, UK: The Boydell Press, 1988.

Jarman, Thomas Leckie. *William Marshal: First Earl of Pembroke*. Oxford: Basil Blackwell, 1930.

Keen, Maurice. *Chivalry*. New Haven, CT: Yale University Press, 1984.

Painter, William. *William Marshal: Knight-Errant, Baron, and Regent of England*. Baltimore: Johns Hopkins Press, 1933. Reprint. Toronto: University of Toronto Press, 1997.

Sources

FOREWARD

p. 9, "the great merits and the honor . . ." Duby, Georges. *William Marshal: the Flower of Chivalry.* New York: Pantheon Books, 1986, p. 29.

p. 10, "The story of his life ought . . ." Gillingham, John. *Thirteenth Century England II.* Edited by P. R. Coss and S. D. Lloyd. Suffolk, UK: The Boydell Press, 1988, p. 2.

CHAPTER ONE

p. 14, "I possess the anvil and hammer . . ." Crosland, Jessie. *William the Marshal.* London: Peter Owen LTD, 1962, pp. 19-20.

p. 14, "William, you will never be harmed by me." Gies, Frances. *The Knight in History.* New York: Harper & Row, 1984, p. 84.

p. 15, "How is my lady mother . . ." ibid.

CHAPTER TWO

p. 25, "In remembrance of Him who ordained you . . ." Gies, op. cit., p. 85.

p. 26, "Give me a crupper . . ." Crouch, David. *William Marshal: Court, Career and Chivalry in the Angevin Empire 1147-1219*. London: Longman, 1994, p. 33.

p. 26, "Oh, but Marshal, what are you saying?" ibid.

CHAPTER THREE

p. 30, "fashioned by a sculptor . . ." Painter, William. *William Marshal: Knight-Errant, Baron, and Regent of England*. Baltimore: Johns Hopkins Press, 1933. Reprint. Toronto: University of Toronto Press, 1997, p. 38.

p. 38, "an acre of land, or . . ." Duby, op. cit., p. 81.

CHAPTER FOUR

p. 42, "You are more worthy . . ." Crosland, op. cit., p. 38.

p. 44, "rushed outside, ran to the groaning . . ." Gies, op. cit., p. 90.

p. 44, "Here, take him to pay . . ." ibid.

p. 45, "Marshal, give me a good horse." Painter, op. cit., p. 41.

CHAPTER FIVE

p. 48, "Dieu, aide au . . ." Painter, op. cit., p. 217.

p. 48, "Grand clamor and great noise . . ." Duby, op. cit., pp. 102-103, 106.

p. 53, "God, how tired I am." Crosland, op. cit., p. 53.

p. 53, "Bridle my horse" ibid.

p. 53, "I am a man." ibid.

p. 53, "I can see that you that are not an animal." ibid.

p. 54, "My son has cost me more than that . . ." Crosland, op. cit., p. 57.

CHAPTER SIX

p. 59, "impressive military peacock." Crouch, op. cit., p. 180.

p. 59, "My lords, of what use . . ."Crosland, op. cit.,p. 59.

p. 60, "Are we an army of . . ." ibid., p. 60.

p. 60, "By God's eyes," Gillingham, John. "War and Chivalry in the History of William the Marshal," *Thirteen Century England II*. Suffolk, UK: The Boydell Press, 1988, p. 5.

p. 60, "We have well avenged our elm . . ." Crosland, op. cit., p. 61.

p. 60, "Bring my shield!" ibid.

p. 61, "I knew only too well that my children . . ." ibid., p. 62.

p. 65, "By the legs of God, Marshal, do not kill me . . ." Painter, op. cit. p. 70.

p. 65, "No, let the devil kill you . . ." ibid.

p. 66, "joyful, sad, remorseful . . ." Crouch, op. cit., p. 58.

p. 66, "Sire, I had no intention of killing you . . ." Duby, op. cit., p. 123.

p. 68, "the good the fair, the wise . . ." Painter, op. cit, p. 76.

CHAPTER SEVEN
p. 74, "Although I have never so afflicted . . ." ibid., p. 73.

p. 75, "Sire, we have only done our duty." Crosland, op. cit., p. 73.

p. 76, "It is not fitting for a man of your rank . . . " Painter, op.cit, p. 111.

p. 77, "Sire, you ought to have been laughing . . ." Crosland, op. cit., p. 81.

CHAPTER EIGHT
p. 79 "a day and a night." Crouch, op. cit., p. 79.

p. 82, "Marshal, I know for certain . . ." Crosland, op. cit., p. 91.

p. 82, "Sire, you know well . . ." ibid.

p. 82, "That is not true . . ." ibid.

p. 83, "Lords! See the countess . . ." Crouch, op. cit., p. 100.

p. 84, "He took no heed of what had gone before. . ." ibid., p. 110.

p. 84, "for the sake of peace," Jarman, Thomas Leckie. *William Marshal: First Earl of Pembroke*. Oxford: Basil Blackwell, 1930, p. 51.

p. 86, "Pray the Marshal to pardon the wrongs . . ." ibid., p. 52.

CHAPTER NINE

p. 87, "Sire," replied the Marshal, "by my soul . . . " Painter, op. cit., p. 192.

p. 88, "Who other, even if there were a thousand of us . . ." Crosland, op. cit., p. 113.

p. 89, "sea without bottom or bank . . ." Painter, op. cit., p. 196.

p. 89, "Your advice is true and good . . ." Crouch, op. cit., p. 119.

p. 91, "Listen to me, all you loyal knights . . ." Crosland, op. cit., p. 120.

p. 92, "as swift as a bird . . ." Jarman, op. cit., p. 62-63.

p. 92, "Dieu aide au . . ." Painter, op. cit., p. 217.

CHAPTER TEN

p. 96, "Sire, I pray the Lord God . . ." Crosland, op. cit., p. 143.

p. 96, "Lords, one of my sons, Anselm . . ." Painter, op. cit.. p. 281.

p. 96, "Ah, Lord, do not do that." ibid.

p. 97, "If only she too were well married . . ." Crosland, op. cit., p. 144.

p. 97, "Lords, look here. I have had . . ." Painter, op. cit., p. 284.

p. 97, "I do not know why it is, but for . . ." ibid., p. 286.

p. 98, "Say no more wretches." Duby, op. cit., p. 19.

p. 98, "I am dying. I commend you . . ." ibid., p. 21.

p. 99, "the best knight in the world." Gillingham, *Thirteenth Century England II*, p. 2.

Index